COLETTE'S SLIM CUISINE

Books by Colette Rossant

THE MOSTLY FRENCH PROCESSOR COOKBOOK
THE AFTER-FIVE GOURMET
COLETTE'S SLIM CUISINE

COLETTE'S SLIM CUISINE

COLETTE ROSSANT

Drawings by James S. Rossant

William Morrow and Company, Inc.
New York

To Jim, my husband,
whose love, imagination, drawings,
and taste buds
have made this book possible.

Library of Congress Cataloging in Publication Data

Rossant, Colette.
Colette's Slim cuisine.

Includes index.
1. Low-calorie diet—Recipes.   I. Title.   II. Title:
Slim cuisine.
RM222.2.R664   1983   641.5'635   83-992
ISBN 0-688-01937-4

Printed in the United States of America

First Edition

1 2 3 4 5 6 7 8 9 10

BOOK DESIGN BY ANTLER & BALDWIN

CONTENTS

INTRODUCTION

I wrote this book for people who, like me, believe that cooking is both an everyday pleasure and an expressive art. The recipes in it are an adventure and a discovery of texture, taste, color, and form. It is not a diet book, but rather a collection of recipes in a new culinary style that I developed for myself and for the countless people who love to cook and love to eat. I wanted to find a new way of cooking for those who want to adapt their family meals, and their style of entertaining, to their awareness of health and weight and the things that modern medicine is telling us. This idea is not incompatible with the idea that cooking is an art.

In these recipes, which I developed for over a year, testing them on my friends and my family, I have tried to convey a sense of discovery and sometimes a sense of mystery. Being interested in Japanese and Chinese culture, I turned to nature for what I felt to be missing from our Western style of cooking and eating. Many of my ideas have come from my knowledge of Chinese and Japanese cuisine—not by imitating their dishes, but from learning how to use their ingredients and spices, mixing them together with my French skills. The recipes became an alliance of East and West that I believe can make a dinner, any dinner, a true adventure.

I wanted to express in the recipes a relationship between the sea and the earth. I also felt food could express abstract concepts, very like paint on a canvas. For example, one concept that intrigued me was food as a series of circles. When you throw a stone into a calm pond, from one small center it forms larger and larger circles. This is how I sometimes imagine a dish—something hidden in the center, with the mystery expanding like a series of circles, ending with a wrapping of seaweed, like water. For example, a chicken breast pounded very thin hiding vegetables cut even smaller, the whole package wrapped in Japanese seaweed. I like to wrap chicken or fish in leaves, hide vegetables in cabbage, and replace the bone of a chicken leg with vegetables.

My ideas have come from exploring images like this and from making new discoveries in the changing world around me. I wanted to play, invent games, be outrageous by combining flavors that would surprise and at the same time stimulate your palate. My outlet for imagination is experimentation—and sometimes the experiments failed. Or sometimes I found myself turning in the opposite direction, away from the complex and mysterious. I sought simpler elements. I went back to the primary ingredients and used them alone, fresh, young, unsurpassed in their taste. I took cauliflower in the spring and simply steamed it, zucchini at their smallest and just boiled them or ate them raw with coarse salt—alliances of earth and water in their purest forms.

The idea of this book also came from my own experience with trying to lose weight. Until the summer of 1980, I had never been overweight; I could have lost a few pounds perhaps, but nothing more than that. At the beginning of that particular summer, I decided to stop smoking. I was about to take a long airplane trip to Africa and decided that once I stepped on the plane, I would have had my last cigarette. During the difficult time of adjustment, I gained twenty pounds.

One night at dinner I was sitting next to a doctor. Our conversation drifted to diets, losing weight, the modern way of living. The doctor, who was interested in both food and weight loss, told me that whenever I ate fat I would gain weight. The way to lose weight was to eliminate as much fat as possible from my diet—to eat fish, lean poultry, veal, and sometimes lamb, no beef and no pork of any kind.

I felt that I could certainly do that, and keeping in mind his advice I set out once again to shed those twenty pounds. I decided that whatever I was to eat, my family would have to eat also. I am a working woman and I don't have time to prepare several different meals at each sitting. After three days of a strict regimen, I couldn't stand the diet, my husband threatened divorce, and my son announced that he no longer wanted to eat dinner at home. The situation was ridiculous.

I started thinking, why can't we eat well, have fun, and lose weight? From that day on, I began to cook differently. I prepared a different meal every night. I made chicken ten different ways, explored all sorts of fish. We had new kinds of vegetables and salads in abundance. I invented new salad dressings and sauces. I used little or no fat in my cooking and managed to make delicious dishes *sans beurre* and *sans* boredom. My family once again enjoyed the evening meal—and at last I was losing some weight.

I found many inspirations for recipes by looking more closely at the markets around me. First, I decided to explore thoroughly all the new vegetable stores. Greengroceries are no longer places where one finds just carrots, celery, cabbage, and green peppers. I found fiddleheads, kohlrabi, strange purple potatoes, spaghetti squash. Walking through Chinatown I discovered winter melon, mile-long string beans, endless new varieties of greens. Suddenly, I saw that not only I but everyone and everything around me was changing. In New York, every neighborhood has a new vegetable store, and these new outlets bring new ingredients into our daily lives. I found endless varieties of green vegetables such as sorrel, Swiss chard, Chinese spinach, green plantain, and jucca and chayote from the Caribbean, taro root, tropical fruits such as passion fruit and mangoes, and vegetables never before seen on our supermarket shelves such as sugar snap peas. I began to remember ideas and ingredients that I had discovered traveling abroad, and I went exploring not only in Chinatown but also to Japanese stores and to every kind of unusual market in the city.

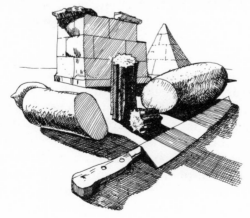

New York markets have so much, I know we are privileged here. Even so, I have included in this book recipes for quite a few of the unusual ingredients I found—especially fresh produce—to show how unfamiliar things can inspire new ideas and also because, if you should be able to find them, too, it may not be easy to find recipes for using them simply and well. Some items, such as bean curd, which was generally unknown until a few years ago, are now common on supermarket shelves all over the country. And I rely very much on a few special but not obscure ingredients—fresh herbs, fresh ginger, sesame seeds, sesame oil.

My discoveries in the marketplace also brought me to an attempt at revolutionizing an especially challenging element of traditional cuisine—sauces. From the Middle Ages to the present, sauces have been important in *haute cuisine*. Escoffier compared a *saucier* to a researcher, to a painter looking for the right blend of color to obtain the right tone. Sauces have been called the mortar that holds the edifice of a great dish together. For me, sauces help express or intensify a dish, like an architect's ornament over a classic window or the outlines in a Roualt painting. But sauces inevitably used to mean butter, cream, all sorts of other rich ingredients. I have turned instead to vegetables for color and texture in making sauces, to bean curd for taste and substance, and to yogurt for the last touch that adds smoothness, a taste of richness to my sauces.

Bean curd, or *tofu*, is one of the ingredients that has helped me most in my new cooking. I started to be interested in it when I discovered that it has been used for centuries by the Chinese and the Japanese and that is is both high in protein and low in calories. One has a deep feeling of coolness eating Japanese bean curd. It is a kind of perfect food, which attracted me and made me want to explore it more thoroughly.

My Egyptian background, where yogurt is to cooking what bean curd is to oriental cuisine, also made me want to make more use of that ingredient. Its slightly sour taste helps to intensify an already present taste, just like salt or pepper. Also, modern technology has helped by making possible yogurt with a low percentage of fat without taking away its creamy taste and texture.

Spices and fresh herbs became even more important to me than they had been before. To make simply cooked foods interesting, I started to experiment with them, and I went out of my way to look for fresh herbs. When I couldn't find them, I grew them myself. Chervil, mint, marjoram, basil, Chinese lemon grass, rosemary, anise, sage, thyme. Tarragon, the king of French herbs, used with chicken or turkey breast gives it a superb flavor; rosemary cooked in a stew adds richness to the meat. Cumin or sesame seeds sprinkled on steamed vegetables gives them an added dimension. Moving away from traditional spices, I started to use Japanese seasonings such as *furikake* (made of ground seaweed and sesame seeds), sesame oil, and spicy hot oil. I turned to Chinatown for soy sauce and discovered that there is more than the usual variety found in supermarkets. A dark, thick soy, mild in taste, called black soy, is marvelous to rub onto chicken before roasting. It gives the chicken a golden color and adds pungency to the meat. Mushroom soy, a thick soy sauce with a strong flavor of mushroom, is excellent for making broth and soups and adds depth to bouillons for jellies. The light-colored soy, saltier than the others, is an excellent dip for fresh ingredients just steamed.

But it was fresh gingerroot that changed the taste of my cooking the most. My first encounter with gingerroot was when I was seventeen in, of all places, *A Thousand and One Nights,* in which I read that ginger had marvelous stimulating properties; it was said to be a cure for troubled love and to prolong life. Later, when I started to explore Japanese cooking, I found that far back in history ginger was considered a food for the gods that also prevented diseases and had the same quality of cure that garlic was known for in the Middle Ages in Europe. When I started to use fresh ginger, its aroma brought back memories of foreign dishes and excited my taste buds. Its pungent taste enhances food and its peppery quality makes the flavor of plainly cooked vegetables, fish, or poultry come alive.

Fresh lemon and lime are also important elements in many of my recipes. Aristophanes wrote that lemon leaves were used to make crowns to be placed on the heads of the immortal gods. We don't think along those lines today, but lemon and lime do transform meat and fish into foods more fit for the gods than they would be otherwise. Lime juice changes an ordinary piece of meat into something that tingles. The zest of lime or lemon grated over steamed vegetables will make the routine become sublime.

Finally, the dessert in this new slim cuisine of mine should usually be fruit, a beautiful fruit. Why fruit only? To end the meal with simplicity. Nothing is more beautiful than a peach, a ripe peach, served on a green leaf as nature intended us to eat it. It reminds me of the *nature morte* of painters. I use fruit often in this way, as the primary ingredient, the star of the show. Or it may also be used as a device, such as a melon used as a serving bowl in which other ingredients are mixed to create another dimension. Or I combine fruits in a magic design—blackberries reflecting, recreating the seeds in a jellied watermelon mousse. If I make more elaborate desserts, fruit is always a part of them. In all seasons of the year, fruit provides the perfect dessert.

PRACTICAL MATTERS

How to Use This Book

The recipes in this book, by themselves, will not make anyone lose weight. You must also use restraint and have a balanced diet. In planning a dinner, for entertaining or any time, one has to be careful in making the selection of the appetizer, the main course, the vegetable or salad, and the dessert. To help you with your choices, a total calorie count is given for each recipe. Some are much higher in calories than others. If you choose an elaborate hors d'oeuvre, then the main course should be something broiled or steamed, served with a light salad or vegetable. If the main course is more substantial and has more calories, then the choice of appetizer should be light. Choose desserts to balance your dinner in the same way. I have included some party desserts that are only reduced in calories, rather than strictly diet conscious.

I hope you will use these recipes, as I do, to entertain your guests and to make food that is interesting, artful, and challenging and in which no one will miss the calories.

Special Ingredients

Fresh herbs: Many markets now carry them—mint, chives, dill, basil. But since this is not true everywhere, you may have to use your ingenuity, as I did. If you have a sunny windowsill, you can actually grow fresh herbs all year long. If you have a garden, plant for the summer as many different ones as you have room for. Many herbs can be dried or frozen. In the spring and summer, basil becomes available in quantity. Remove the leaves from the stems, wash the leaves very carefully, and let them dry in a colander until all their moisture has evaporated. Then freeze them in plastic bags; you will have "fresh" basil in the winter.

Dried herbs: Although fresh herbs are unmatched for their flavor and zest, dried herbs of good quality are a necessity. They need to be measured with some care, so many of the recipes specify an amount for dried herbs. But use chopped fresh herbs to taste instead—double the amount given for the dried—whenever you can.

Fresh gingerroot: This is available all year round in supermarkets as well as specialty stores. If at all possible, avoid the dried or powdered varieties. Select a piece of gingerroot carefully; the skin and cut edges must not be crinkled and dried out. Ginger will keep longer if it is stored in the refrigerator; or it may be peeled, cut in chunks, and stored in rice wine, tightly covered.

Sesame seeds: There are two types, black and white. The white sesame seeds should be toasted before use; see page 220. Most of the time, I use the black sesame seeds. I find them tastier, and you need very little. Half a teaspoon sprinkled on a steamed cauliflower is marvelous; a little bit underneath the skin of a chicken breast will change its taste. Black sesame seeds do not need to be toasted, but you may if you want to sharpen their flavor.

Bean curd or tofu: There are two kinds available now: the soft bean curd, which is excellent for sauces, and the regular variety, which is better to use to bind a filling where flour and butter would normally be used.

Special seasonings: I am particularly fond of sesame oil. It is found in most health-food stores. A quarter of a teaspoon will add an interesting new taste to a whole dish. Dried seaweed, also available in health-food stores and in Japanese markets, is very good for lining a steamer and to give a surprising new flavor to cooking. I like it for wrapping meats, to replace the usual sautéing or frying. Oriental hot oil, used a few drops at a time, serves the same purpose as cayenne pepper, but I think more subtly.

You will notice that I do not give amounts for salt and pepper. They are a matter of taste. But it is well known to everyone by now that we should cut back on the amount of salt we use. I recommend that you learn to use less and less. You will discover flavors in food you never knew were there when they were oversalted! Be especially careful not to oversalt a dish that contains soy sauce. In fact, always look at the ingredients before starting to cook; when one of them is already salty, you may need no additional salt at all. And I do like to season the component parts of some recipes separately; this, too, requires restraint. Pepper is not a problem and is certainly a matter of taste. I *always* use a pepper grinder.

The Food Processor and the Steamer

A food processor is twentieth century; it is the machine age, high tech, invading our kitchens. It will cut, shred, slice, purée—change the shape and even the flavor of ingredients. So it must never become the master, but always remain the helper. The simple steamer is the opposite of the processor. It preserves the best in ingredients and helps to keep intact not only the taste but also the shape and color of foods. It represents health, nature—water, purity—unaltered.

Both these tools are essential and they are complementary. In this book, many of the ingredients must be cooked quickly—steamed or sautéed—with no fat or very little. Therefore they will often need to be evenly sliced or shredded in the processor. And the processor is most essential for puréeing—to make soups, sauces, and the fillings in many recipes that would be laborious and less successful without a processor. (Occasionally I also use an electric blender for small quantities of ingredients.)

Bamboo steamer: This is the kind I always use. I buy them in Chinatown and they are now also found in the better kitchen-housewares stores. They are handmade and quite beautiful; you can use them to serve the food after it is cooked. Several tiers, or racks, can be stacked on top of each other with one domed bamboo lid on top. Bamboo steamers are made in many different sizes. The most practical are 12 inches in diameter for an average-size stove and 14 inches for a larger stove.

Bamboo steamers are not sold with their own pot to hold the boiling water underneath. The Chinese use a wok. I use an enameled cast-iron skillet about 1 inch larger in diameter than the steamer. (If you use a wok, that wok can be used only for steaming, as the water removes the wok's patina.)

To use the bamboo steamer: When the ingredients are small, such as peas or a julienne of vegetables, line the steamer with lettuce or cabbage leaves. When steaming fish, line the steamer with a Handy Wipe so that the odor of the fish will not be absorbed by the bamboo.

Pour 2 cups of boiling water from a tea kettle into the skillet, place the steamer over the water, and put on the lid. The water must not touch the food. Use medium heat under the skillet to keep the water simmering. You may need to add more water for longer-cooking foods—8 or 10 minutes or more. Pour it in slowly at the side, between the steamer and the rim of the skillet. Remove the lid carefully (steam can burn) to check for doneness. When the steaming is done, turn off the heat, and immediately remove the lid. The food will continue to cook if the lid stays on.

Remember that foods cook very rapidly in a steamer.

Aluminum steamer: These are available with two or three perforated tiers and a dome-shaped lid. The tiers fit on top of a deep pot which holds the water. These steamers are made 11 inches, 13 inches, and 15 inches in diameter.

When using an aluminum steamer, always line the tiers with lettuce or cabbage leaves to avoid any metallic taste. When steaming delicate dishes, such as custard or fish, wrap the lid from the underside with a cloth napkin so that the steam that condenses in the lid will not fall back on the food. An advantage of this steamer is that the pot holds a large amount of water.

There are also small metal steamer baskets made of stainless steel, about 5½ inches in diameter at the base with perforated "leaves" that fan out around it. The steamer rests on three legs to hold the food above the water in an ordinary saucepan. There is a metal post in the center to lift the entire steamer out of the pot. This steamer is fine for small items for one person.

COLD HORS D'OEUVRE & FIRST COURSES

Cherry Tomatoes Stuffed with String-Bean Purée

1 pound string beans
½ cup chicken consommé
salt and pepper
2 teaspoons chopped fresh mint
2 containers cherry tomatoes (about 2 pounds)
fresh mint leaves for garnish

Trim the string beans. Steam them, covered, for 8 minutes. Place the beans in a blender or a food processor, add ¼ cup of the consommé, and purée. Add more consommé if the purée seems too dense. Remove to a bowl and add salt and pepper to taste and the chopped mint.

Wash and drain the cherry tomatoes. With a sharp knife cut off the top of each tomato. With an espresso spoon remove the seeds. Fill with the string-bean purée. Serve on a platter garnished with fresh mint leaves.

Serve with drinks or as an appetizer with Mushroom Pâté (page 20).

Yield: 10 to 15 servings
Total calories: 340

Bay Scallops with Red Lumpfish Caviar

This is a very simple recipe. What makes it interesting is the way it is served. The scallops are strung on toothpicks, with a melon ball at one end. They are set in a circle on a round serving platter. In the center is a small bowl filled with red lumpfish caviar to be used as the dip.

1 pound bay scallops
juice of 4 limes
2-ounce jar red lumpfish caviar
1 cantaloupe
2 limes, sliced very thin, for garnish

bamboo skewers

The bay scallops should marinate for 24 hours. Place them in a deep bowl, add the lime juice, cover, and refrigerate.

The next day, cut the cantaloupe in two and seed it. With a melon-ball cutter, make as many small balls as you can. For each toothpick, start with a melon ball, then add 3 to 4 scallops. Place them in a circle on a round platter. In the center place the jar of caviar, and garnish the platter with very thin slices of lime. Refrigerate until ready to serve with drinks.

Yield: 10 to 12 servings
Total calories: 630

Beets Stuffed with Black Lumpfish Caviar

This is excellent to serve with drinks or to add to a buffet.

16-ounce can small whole beets
salt and pepper
¼ cup chopped parsley
2-ounce jar black lumpfish caviar
1 bunch watercress
sliced limes for garnish

Drain the beets. Cut a small slice off the bottom of each one so that the beets can stand. Then with an espresso spoon make holes on the tops big enough to hold about an espresso-spoonful of the caviar. Sprinkle the beets with salt and pepper, roll them in chopped parsley, and then fill each cavity with caviar.

Line a serving platter with watercress, arrange the beets in circles in the center, and garnish with lime slices. Serve very cold.

Yield: 6 to 8 servings
Total calories: 180

Mushroom Pâté

>2 pounds white mushrooms + 6 mushrooms for garnish
>2 envelopes unflavored gelatin
>2 bean curd cakes
>3 eggs + 1 yolk
>2 tablespoons dried tarragon
>salt and pepper
>2 limes
>parsley for garnish
>Stewed Tomatoes (page 224)
>
>1-quart loaf pan

Preheat the oven to 375°.

The success of this pâté depends on how dry the mushrooms are; they have very few or almost no calories, but they hold a lot of water. Wash the mushrooms rapidly, drain in a colander, and then pat dry with paper towels. In a food processor purée the 2 pounds of mushrooms with their stems. Pour the purée into a fine sieve set over a bowl and let it stand for 1 hour; reserve the water that drains off.

In a small saucepan soak the gelatin in 4 tablespoons of the mushroom water. Heat the mixture and stir until the gelatin is dissolved.

In the food processor purée together the gelatin mixture, bean curd, eggs, and tarragon. Run the machine until all the ingredients are well puréed.

Wash and cut in two the 6 remaining mushrooms. Sprinkle with salt and pepper and the juice of ½ a lime. Set aside.

Mix together the mushroom and bean curd purées. Correct seasoning with salt and pepper. Pour ½ the mixture into a loaf pan. (It is best to use disposable aluminum loaf pans; the sides can be cut away and the pâté is then easily removed.) Place the marinated mushrooms in the center and cover with the remaining purée.

Cover the pan with foil, and make a hole in the center for steam to escape. Bake in the 375° oven in a *bain-marie* (a pan of hot water) for 45 minutes. Remove from the oven and cool. Refrigerate until ready to serve. (The pâté can be kept for a week.)

Unmold the pâté carefully, cut in slices, and serve on individual plates. Garnish with parsley, Stewed Tomatoes, and a slice of lime. (Or, instead, serve Cherry Tomatoes Stuffed with String-Bean Purée, page 18.)

Yield: 10 servings
Total calories: 1,035

Pâté Calvin as in Calvin Trillin

I made this pâté for Calvin and my husband. They both complained that we, their wives, were feeding them too much. But on the other hand, they wanted an appetizer for dinner, "A pâté, maybe?" I tried several times and finally came up with this idea—two colors of vegetables with something in the center to tie them together. If your guests don't eat meat, use some shrimp, fish, etc. I used chicken livers. The pâté must be refrigerated for at least 24 hours.

1 bunch broccoli (1½ pounds)
4 eggs
2 tablespoons dried thyme
salt and pepper
12-ounce can artichoke bottoms
4 envelopes unflavored gelatin
2 tablespoons cold water
juice of 1 lemon
6 chicken livers
1 tablespoon dried tarragon
parsley for garnish
1 lime, sliced, for garnish

1-quart loaf pan or terrine

Preheat the oven to 450°.

Trim the broccoli, cut off most of the stems, and steam the green tops, covered, for 5 minutes. Remove to a food processor.

Purée the broccoli with 2 eggs, 1 tablespoon of the thyme, and salt and pepper to taste. Set aside in a bowl.

Drain the artichoke bottoms and purée in the food processor with the remaining eggs, remaining thyme, and salt and pepper. Set aside in a bowl.

Soak the gelatin in 2 tablespoons cold water, then add the lemon juice and heat over simmering hot water until the gelatin is totally dissolved. Add ½ the gelatin mixture to the broccoli purée and mix well. Add the remaining gelatin mixture to the artichoke purée and mix well.

Steam the chicken livers, covered, for 5 minutes. Remove to a bowl and sprinkle with salt, pepper, and 1 tablespoon tarragon. Toss carefully.

Line a terrine with foil (it will help you later to unmold the pâté). Pour in the artichoke purée first. Then place the chicken livers in a line in the center. Finish with the broccoli purée and cover with foil.

Bake in the 450° oven in a *bain-marie* (a pan of hot water) for 20 minutes. Remove from the oven and cool. Refrigerate with a weight on top, such as 2 cans, for 24 hours. Unmold on a platter and garnish with parsley and lime slices.

Yield: 8 to 12 servings
Total calories: 990

Cecile's Sesame Bread and Crackers

I am not a good baker for I have no patience and I don't understand chemistry, or at least this is what Cecile, my youngest daughter, tells me. One day I was attempting to make crackers when she pushed me out of the kitchen and took over. Her crackers and her bread, made of the same dough, were the hit of the dinner.

1 package dry yeast
1 cup hot water
1 teaspoon sugar

3 cups whole wheat flour
1 teaspoon salt
2½ tablespoons olive oil
¼ cup black sesame seeds
2 teaspoons curry powder
1 teaspoon cumin
Pepper
½ tablespoon butter for the cooky sheet

8-by-4-by-2½-inch loaf pan

BREAD:

Dissolve the yeast in the hot water, add the sugar, mix well, and let the mixture sit for about 10 minutes or until it begins to bubble.

In a bowl mix the flour with the salt, then pour in the yeast mixture. Beat with a wooden spoon until all the mixture has been incorporated in the flour. Turn the dough out onto a floured board and knead with your hands for 10 minutes. (This step could be done with a food processor, but the bread has a better texture if it is kneaded by hand.)

Grease a bowl with some of the olive oil, place the dough in it, and let it rise, covered, in a warm place until it doubles in bulk, about 45 minutes.

Punch the dough down. Cut off ⅓ of the dough and set aside to make crackers. Mix the sesame seeds with the curry and cumin, adding some salt and pepper. Roll out the dough on the floured board in a long rectangle. Brush it with olive oil and sprinkle with some of the sesame seed mixture. From one narrow end roll the bread like a jelly roll and tuck the ends under. Grease a loaf pan with olive oil, place the roll in the pan, seam side down, and make two diagonal slits across the top. Let it rise for 30 minutes in a warm place.

Preheat the oven to 400°.

Bake the bread for 45 minutes or until golden brown. Serve hot or at room temperature, with a pâté before dinner, or with dinner.

Total calories: 1,445

CRACKERS:

Preheat the oven to 400°.

Butter a cooky sheet. Roll out the remaining dough about ⅛ inch thick and the size of the cooky sheet. Line the cooky sheet with the dough, brush with olive oil, and sprinkle with sesame seeds. Press the seeds into the dough. Bake in the 400° oven for 20 minutes or until golden brown. Cut into 2-inch squares and serve with drinks or cheese.

Yield: About 20 to 24 crackers
Total calories: 720

Tomato Bread

This unusual, lovely looking bread was served to me in Tanzania by an Australian friend who in turn had gotten the recipe from a Kenyan friend. Sliced thin, it is excellent for sandwiches stuffed with watercress or cucumbers and low-fat farmer's cheese.

1¼ cups warm water
1¼ teaspoons flour
1¼ teaspoons dry yeast
6 cups unbleached white flour
2 teaspoons salt
2 teaspoons paprika
¾ cup tomato juice
3 tablespoons oil
½ tablespoon butter for the mold
1 tablespoon milk
poppy seeds for garnish

8-by-4-inch disposable aluminum-foil pound-cake pan

In a blender place the water, 1¼ teaspoons flour, and the yeast. Run the machine until the ingredients are well mixed. Remove to a bowl and leave for 5 minutes to allow the yeast to work.

In a food processor place the 6 cups flour, salt, paprika,

tomato juice, and oil. Run the machine until all the ingredients are mixed, then add the yeast mixture and mix again. Place the dough in a large plastic bag, tie, and let rise in a warm place for 1 hour, or until the dough has doubled in size.

Turn out the dough onto a floured board. Butter the pound-cake pan and place the dough in it. Place the pan back in the plastic bag and let the dough rise again for 20 minutes more.

Preheat the oven to 400°. Brush the top of the loaf with the milk, press on the poppy seeds, and bake in the 400° oven for 40 minutes. Unmold and let cool.

Slice thin to serve with soup or use for sandwiches.

Total calories: 3,210

Terrine of Chicken with Blueberries

The first time I tried this recipe I overcooked the blueberries and I ended up with a nondescript purple pâté. The secret is to marinate the chicken pieces for at least 12 hours and to just heat, not cook, the blueberries. Serve this terrine with a bowl of more fresh blueberries.

1 large roasting chicken (about 5 pounds)
2 shallots, chopped
2 garlic cloves, chopped
salt and pepper
1¼ cups dry white wine
1 cup dry vermouth
1 cup chicken bouillon
1 bay leaf
2 tablespoons dried tarragon
2 envelopes unflavored gelatin
2 tablespoons cold water
1 pound blueberries

Bone the chicken or have the butcher do it for you. (If neither is possible, cut the chicken in small pieces, follow the recipe, and bone it when it is cooked and cool.)

In a large bowl place the chicken meat, shallots, garlic, and salt and pepper. Add the white wine and vermouth, mix well, and refrigerate for at least 12 hours.

The next day, remove the chicken meat from the marinade and place it in a 5-quart saucepan. Strain the marinade, add to the chicken, and add the bouillon, bay leaf, and tarragon. Bring to a boil, lower the heat, and simmer, covered, for 30 minutes, or until the chicken is cooked. Remove the chicken to a bowl. Chill the cooking liquid and then degrease it.

Soak the gelatin in 2 tablespoons of cold water. Heat the cooking liquid again, add the gelatin, and mix well until all the gelatin is dissolved. Add ½ the blueberries and turn off the heat. Cool. Add the chicken meat. (Bone the chicken now if it was cooked with the bones.) Mix lightly and correct the seasoning.

Pour the mixture into an oval terrine or serving bowl. Refrigerate for a couple of hours. Serve sliced, with the remaining fresh blueberries.

Yield: 6 to 8 servings
Total calories: 1,075

Chicken Terrine with Leeks

2 pounds leeks
1 large onion
3 cloves
2 turnips
1 green pepper
3 carrots
2 garlic cloves
½ tablespoon dried thyme
3 parsley sprigs
10 peppercorns
3-pound chicken

1 tablespoon coarse salt
2 envelopes unflavored gelatin
2 tablespoons cold water
salt and pepper
parsley for garnish

6-cup disposable aluminum-foil loaf pan

Trim and wash the leeks and tie with a string. (Cut off most of the green part; it can be used to make soup.) Peel the onion and stick the cloves in it. Peel the turnips. Seed and cut up the pepper. Cut the carrots into 2-inch pieces. Peel the garlic and crush with the flat of a knife. Tie the thyme, parsley, and peppercorns in a piece of cheesecloth.

Remove the chicken's heart, liver, and giblets, rinse and pat dry. Rinse the chicken under cold water and pat dry. Place liver, heart, and giblets inside chicken.

In a large soup kettle place the chicken, onion, and 1 tablespoon coarse salt. Cover with cold water, bring to a boil, reduce the heat, and simmer, skimming the surface from time to time. After 10 minutes, add the vegetables and the herbs. Cook, simmering, for 45 minutes or until chicken is done. Remove it to a platter to cool. Strain the bouillon into a large bowl.

In a food processor place the liver, heart, and giblets. Add the vegetables (remove the string from the leeks). Discard the herbs. Run the machine until all the ingredients are puréed.

Soak the gelatin in 2 tablespoons cold water, then add 2 cups of the chicken bouillon and stir with a wooden spoon. Pour the gelatin mixture into a small saucepan and heat gently until the gelatin is totally dissolved. Add to the puréed vegetables. Cool.

Remove the skin from the chicken and discard. Cut the chicken meat into thin strips about 3 inches long. Line the bottom of the pâté pan with some of the chicken and sprinkle with salt and pepper. Cover with some of the vegetable-gelatin mixture. Make more layers in the same way until all the chicken is used. Cover with foil and refrigerate overnight.

To serve, dip for a second in hot water and unmold onto a platter. Garnish with parsley and serve with either Fresh Tomato Sauce (page 225) or Parsley Sauce (page 224).

Yield: 8 servings
Total calories: 1,750

Turkey Terrine

1 pound boned turkey breast, cut in 2-inch cubes
2 eggs
2 shallots, chopped
2 tablespoons yogurt
2 tablespoons chopped parsley
salt and pepper
2 tablespoons brandy
1 pound boned chicken breast
14-ounce can sweet red peppers, cut into strips
1 bay leaf
2 envelopes unflavored gelatin
2 tablespoons cold water
2 cups chicken bouillon
watercress for garnish

8-by-4-inch disposable aluminum-foil pound-cake pan

Preheat the oven to 375°.

Chop the cubed turkey breast in a food processor. In a bowl combine the chopped turkey, eggs, chopped shallots, yogurt, parsley, and salt and pepper to taste. Mix well. Add the brandy, mix again, and set aside.

Flatten the chicken breasts and cut them lengthwise into strips 2 inches wide. Line the pound-cake pan with ⅓ of the turkey mixture. Place on top ½ the chicken breast meat. Sprinkle with salt and pepper and strips of sweet red peppers. Cover with ½ the remaining turkey, all the remaining chicken, and then the last of the turkey. Place a bay leaf on top.

Cover with foil and bake in a *bain-marie* (a pan of hot water) in the 375° oven for 1 hour. Remove from the oven and cool.

Make the jelly. In a bowl soak the gelatin in 2 tablespoons of cold water. In a small saucepan heat the chicken bouillon, add the gelatin, and mix well until all the gelatin is dissolved. Cool, then pour over the terrine. Refrigerate for 24 hours.

Serve sliced and garnished with watercress.

Yield: 8 servings
Total calories: 1,615

Terrine of Halibut

This terrine can be prepared a day or two in advance. Serve it with a tomato salad. It is a very festive dish and very low in calories.

1½ quarts water
1 carrot, sliced
2 celery stalks, cut in 1-inch pieces
1 onion stuck with a clove
1 bay leaf
5 peppercorns
salt
3½ pounds halibut fillets
2 envelopes unflavored gelatin
3 limes, sliced thin
1 bunch fresh mint (25 to 30 perfect leaves)
1 cup yogurt
juice of ½ lemon
2 tablespoons chopped parsley

1-quart mold (round, or a fish-shaped mold)

Wash the fish, pat dry, and set aside.

Make the court-bouillon. In a large saucepan place the 1½ quarts of water and the carrot, celery, onion, bay leaf, peppercorns, and salt. Bring to a boil, then lower the heat and simmer for 15 minutes.

Add the fish to the court-bouillon and poach for 8 minutes, or until the fish easily flakes with a fork. Remove to a platter with a slotted spoon.

Strain the court-bouillon. In a bowl soak the gelatin in a little cold water. Add the gelatin to 2½ cups of the court-bouillon, and heat until it is completely dissolved. Pour a thin layer of this aspic into the mold and refrigerate for 10 minutes. Slice the limes and decorate the bottom of the mold with the best slices. Pour in some more aspic and refrigerate until it sets. Then arrange the fish in the mold. Add ½ the mint, then pour in the remaining gelatin, and refrigerate for 24 hours.

Beat the yogurt with the lemon juice and add the chopped parsley and salt and pepper to taste.

Unmold the fish onto a round platter, garnish with the remaining whole leaves of mint, and serve with the yogurt sauce.

Yield: 6 to 8 servings
Total calories: 990

Sea Bass Terrine with Green Peas

1/3 cup hot milk
4 slices white bread
2 pounds sea bass fillets
4 eggs
1/2 cup yogurt
1 tablespoon butter
1/2 pound fresh green peas, shelled
2 tablespoons dried tarragon
salt and pepper
1/2 pound shrimp, shelled and deveined
1 lemon for garnish
2 cups Fresh Tomato Sauce (page 225)

2-quart oblong terrine

Heat the milk. Remove the crust from the bread; cut the bread into small pieces, place in a bowl, and pour the hot milk over it. Cut 2 pieces, lengthwise and about 1 inch wide, from the fish fillets and set aside.

In a food processor place the remaining fish and the bread, eggs and yogurt. Run the machine until all the ingredients are pureed. Set aside in a bowl. In a skillet, melt the butter and when it is hot, add the peas and sauté for 3 minutes. Add the tarragon and salt and pepper, and mix well. Remove the peas from the heat and add to the fish mixture. Mix well with a wooden spoon. Cut the shrimp in two, sprinkle with salt and pepper, and add to the fish mixture. Mix well and correct the seasoning.

Preheat the oven to 375°.

Line the terrine with foil; the foil must be large enough to rise at least 4 inches above the rim of the terrine all around. Spread the bottom of the terrine with half the fish mixture. Place on top the 2 strips of fish, and cover with the remaining fish mixture. Fold the edges of the foil over and cover the terrine with another piece of foil. Bake in a *bain-marie* (a pan of hot water) in the 375° oven for 1 hour.

Remove from the oven, cool, and refrigerate overnight. To serve, carefully remove the top piece of foil, unmold the terrine onto a platter, and peel off the remaining foil. Garnish with thin slices of lemon and serve with the Fresh Tomato Sauce.

Yield: 8 servings
Total calories: 2,280

Scrod and Tomato Terrine

1¾ pounds scrod fillets + 1 fish head or tail
1 quart water
1 onion stuck with a clove
1 carrot, sliced
2 thyme sprigs
12 ounces tomato paste or 2 small cans
4 eggs
1 soft bean curd cake
2 tablespoons yogurt
10 fresh basil leaves
salt and pepper
4 mushrooms, sliced
Boston lettuce for garnish
Parsley Sauce (page 224)

1½-quart oblong mold

Make the court-bouillon. In a large saucepan place the fish head, 1 quart water, the onion, and sliced carrot. Add the thyme, bring to a boil, reduce the heat, and simmer for 10 minutes. Wash and pat dry the fish. Poach in the simmering court-bouillon for 5 minutes, then carefully remove to a platter to cool.

Preheat the oven to 425°.

In a food processor mix together the tomato paste, eggs, bean curd, yogurt, 8 of the basil leaves, and salt and pepper. Run the machine until all the ingredients are puréed. Pour ½ the egg-tomato mixture into the mold, then carefully place the fish fillets in the center. Arrange the mushroom slices on top and sprinkle with salt and pepper. Add the remaining egg-tomato mixture. Cover with foil, then bake in a *bain-marie* (a pan of hot water) in the 425° oven for about 40 minutes.

Remove from the oven, cool, then refrigerate for 4 hours. Unmold onto a bed of lettuce, garnish with the remaining basil leaves, and serve with the Parsley Sauce.

Yield: 6 to 8 servings
Total calories: 1,275

Fish Pâté with Tomatoes and Sage

two 1-pound cans stewed whole tomatoes
4 garlic cloves
1½ pounds fish fillets (flounder, striped bass, etc.)
6 eggs
1 cup fresh basil leaves
2 tablespoons chopped fresh sage
salt and pepper
3 drops Tabasco
1 tablespoon olive oil for the mold
3 fresh tomatoes, sliced, for garnish
parsley for garnish

1-quart mold (round, or a fish-shaped mold)

Preheat the oven to 450°.

Drain the stewed tomatoes, cut each tomato in two, and remove the seeds. Peel and chop the garlic.

In a food processor, place the fish fillets, stewed tomatoes, eggs, garlic, basil, and sage. Run the machine until all the ingredients are puréed. Add salt, pepper, and Tabasco. Mix well. Oil the mold. Pour the mixture in the mold. Bake in a *bain-marie* (a pan of hot water) at 450° for about 40 minutes, or until a small skewer inserted comes out clean.

Unmold on a round platter. Garnish with parsley and fresh sliced tomatoes. Serve right away.

Yield: 6 servings
Total calories: 1,350

Small Shrimp Pâtés

¾ pound small shrimp in the shell
½ pound fish fillets (flounder, striped bass, etc.)
1 anchovy fillet
6 ounces cottage cheese (1% fat)
¼ teaspoon cayenne pepper
pinch of nutmeg
salt and pepper
1 lemon, sliced, for garnish
2 tablespoons capers for garnish

6 round ramekins

Shell the shrimp, devein, and cut in small pieces. Place the shrimp in a saucepan, cover with cold water, and bring to a boil. Reduce the heat and simmer for 5 minutes. With a slotted spoon remove the shrimp to a bowl.

Add the fish to the saucepan and simmer for 5 minutes. Remove with a spatula to the bowl of a food processor. Add the anchovy fillet and the cottage cheese, and run the machine until all the ingredients are puréed.

Remove the purée to a bowl, add the cayenne, nutmeg, and salt and pepper to taste. Then add the shrimp, mix well, and divide the mixture among 6 ramekins. Garnish each with a lemon slice and a few capers and refrigerate until ready to serve.

Yield: 6 servings
Total calories: 580

Artichokes and Mussels

Years ago we rented a house on Cape Cod. From Monday to Friday the children (four of them) and I were all alone. Having discovered a bed of mussels under the stone piers of our town's small harbor, every day we ate mussels. We ate them Italian style, French, Chinese, etc., until we ran out of recipes. One day I thought of trying to stuff artichokes with mussels and found out that these two ingredients worked beautifully together. The leaves are dipped in the mussel juice, then the artichoke's bottom is eaten with the mussels.

4 artichokes
1 or 2 lemons
1 tablespoon salt
1 quart fresh mussels in their shells
1 cup dry white wine
2 garlic cloves, chopped
4 tablespoons chopped parsley
pepper

Wash the artichokes under cold running water. Slice the stems to within ½ inch of the bottoms and remove any small withered leaves. Slice about 1 inch off the tops with a kitchen scissors and cut off ½ inch of the surrounding large leaves.

In a kettle of boiling water, place the artichokes and ½ a lemon. Add 1 tablespoon salt, bring to a boil, and boil slowly for 25 minutes or until a leaf comes off easily. Drain and let cool until ready to use.

Meanwhile, wash and scrub the mussels. Remove the beard that is sometimes attached to mussels. Soak in cold water for ½ hour, changing the water from time to time. In a large kettle, place the mussels, white wine, chopped garlic, 2 tablespoons of the chopped parsley, and sprinkle with pepper. Cook over high heat, covered, shaking the pan from time to time, until the mussels open (about 8 to 10 minutes). Discard any that have not opened.

With a slotted spoon remove the mussels to a bowl to cool. Strain the juice through a very fine sieve and reserve. Remove the mussels from their shells.

Pull out the center cone of each artichoke and with a tea-spoon remove the choke. Fill the cavities with mussels, set the artichokes on a platter, and sprinkle with the remaining parsley. Put back the cones, upside down. Correct the seasoning of the mussel juice, adding more lemon juice and maybe some salt. Pour some over the artichokes and serve the rest in a sauceboat.

Yield: 4 servings
Total calories: 540

Mussels and Shredded Carrots in Aspic

1 quart fresh mussels in their shells
2 garlic cloves, chopped
pepper
½ cup water
4 large carrots
salt
2 tablespoons fresh tarragon or 1 tablespoon dried tarragon
1 tablespoon lemon juice
3 envelopes unflavored gelatin
6 pitted black olives
2 lemons, sliced, for garnish

1-quart round mold

Wash and scrub the mussels and soak in cold water for ½ hour, changing the water from time to time. In a large kettle place the mussels and the chopped garlic. Sprinkle with pepper and add ½ cup water. Cover and steam, shaking the kettle from time to time, until the mussels open (about 8 to 10 minutes). Discard any that have not opened.

Remove the mussels with a slotted spoon to a bowl to cool. Strain the liquid through a very fine sieve and reserve.

Shred the carrots with the fine shredding blade of a food pro-cessor. Remove the carrots to a bowl. Add salt and pepper and the tarragon, and lemon juice. Mix well.

Measure the mussel liquid, pour into a pot, and add enough

water to make 4 cups. Soak the gelatin in a little of the mussel liquid, add to the pot, and slowly bring to a boil, stirring all the while. Let this aspic mixture cool.

Remove the mussels from the shells. Slice the black olives and place in the bottom of the mold. Pour in some of the aspic, enough to cover the bottom of the mold, and put in the freezer for 5 minutes or until it sets. Then arrange the mussels in the mold in an even layer and spread the shredded carrots over them. Pour in the remaining aspic, cover with foil, and refrigerate for a couple of hours.

To unmold, dip for a second in hot water. Turn out onto a round serving platter and garnish with lemon slices.

Yield: 6 to 8 servings
Total calories: 570

Carpaccio

Carpaccio is very thin slices of beef, so thin they are almost transparent, marinated and eaten raw with capers and anchovies. You must ask the butcher to slice the beef in the sirloin. Then you must flatten it further between two sheets of foil with the back of a heavy skillet.

> *6 slices beef sirloin, cut very thin (¼ pound in all)*
> *2 tablespoons olive oil*
> *1 green pepper*
> *juice of 2 limes*
> *3 tablespoons capers*
> *freshly ground pepper*

After having flattened each slice of beef, dip a brush in olive oil and paint the slices. Refrigerate for 1 hour.

Remove the seeds from the green pepper, and cut into very thin strips (about ⅛ inch thick). Heat 1 tablespoon olive oil in a skillet and sauté the green peppers for 3 minutes. Remove to a paper towel. On each individual plate place a slice of beef; garnish with the green pepper, pour 1 teaspoon lime juice on each slice, and add some capers and freshly ground pepper. Serve with dry protein toast cut in triangles.

Yield: 6 servings
Total calories: 660

Celery Root with Anchovies and Capers

When I was a child, we sometimes vacationed in Hendaye, on the Atlantic coast of France. One year, just after the war, we spent a summer there. Food was scarce and we often went fishing on the piers of Hendaye. There I met the son of a tuna fisherman. We became friends and they would take me along for days at a time when they went fishing. For lunch we would have radishes and fresh, small anchovies, raw, with salt sprinkled on bread. The best lunches I have ever had! Here is a recipe that is derived from memories of those lunches.

2 large celery roots
1 cup Soy Vinegar Dressing (page 220)
2-ounce can anchovies, drained
3 tablespoons capers
yolks of 2 hard-boiled eggs
1 bunch watercress for garnish
1 lemon for garnish

Peel the celery root and cut it into slices about ½ inch thick. Drop the slices into boiling water for 1 minute and drain immediately. Run cold water over the celery slices to refresh them, drain, and arrange the slices in a bowl. Cover with the Soy Vinegar Dressing. Refrigerate overnight or for at least a couple of hours, turning the slices from time to time.

Arrange 2 to 3 slices of celery root, drained, on each serving plate. Chop the drained anchovies coarsely. Spread some of the anchovies on each slice and sprinkle with capers. Push the egg yolks through a very fine sieve and sprinkle over all. Garnish with watercress and slices of lemon.

Yield: 6 servings
Total calories: 530

Grapefruit with Horseradish

2 large pink grapefruit
½ cup yogurt
1 lime
½ teaspoon grated horseradish
2-ounce jar red lumpfish caviar

Cut the grapefruit in two. With a grapefruit knife remove the fruit and put in a bowl. With a sharp knife remove all the inside skin of the grapefruit shells.

With a fork beat together the yogurt and the juice of ½ the lime. Fold in the grapefruit and add the grated horseradish. Toss well and pile into the grapefruit shells. Sprinkle with the lumpfish caviar and serve garnished with the rest of the lime, sliced.

Yield: 4 servings
Total calories: 390

Cucumber Mousse for a Hot Summer Night

This mousse is like a breath of fresh cool air. Easy to make, it needs no cooking.

1 Chinese cucumber (see Note)
salt
½ cup chopped fresh mint leaves
1 large garlic clove

2 eggs, separated
½ cup yogurt
½ pound cottage cheese (1% fat)
pepper
2 envelopes unflavored gelatin
3 tablespoons cold water
chopped mint for garnish

1-quart round mold

Peel the cucumber and cut it in half crosswise. Set aside a piece to slice for garnish. Cut the remaining pieces in half lengthwise, remove the seeds, and grate the cucumber, using the large holes of a hand grater. Sprinkle with salt and set aside for 10 minutes.

Wash the mint. Set aside some leaves for garnish. Peel the garlic. Drain the cucumber, pressing with your hands to remove all the water. In a food processor place the cucumber, mint, garlic, egg yolks, yogurt, and cottage cheese. Run the machine until all the ingredients are puréed. Remove to a bowl and correct the seasoning with salt and pepper.

In a small bowl soak the gelatin in 3 tablespoons of cold water. Then place the bowl in a saucepan of simmering water. Stir the gelatin until it is totally dissolved and then add it to the cucumber purée.

Beat the egg whites until stiff. Gently fold the cucumber mixture into the egg whites. Pour the mixture into a mold and refrigerate for 4 hours.

To unmold, dip in hot water and turn out onto a round platter. Garnish the top of the mousse with slices of reserved cucumber and sprinkle with chopped mint.

Yield: 8 servings
Total calories: 460

NOTE: Chinese cucumber is a very long cucumber, about 2 inches in diameter, that has a very small center of seeds. It is now found in most American greengroceries.

Cold Tomato Mousse

5 large ripe tomatoes
1 small onion
10 basil leaves
½ pound cottage cheese (1% fat)
2 eggs, separated
½ cup + 2 tablespoons yogurt
1 tablespoon tomato paste
½ teaspoon sugar
salt and pepper
2 envelopes unflavored gelatin
2 tablespoons cold water

1-quart round mold

Dip 4 tomatoes in boiling water and cool under running water. Peel, quarter, and seed. Set aside remaining tomato for garnish. Peel the onion. Wash and pat dry the basil; set aside 3 leaves for garnish.

In a food processor place the tomatoes, onion, basil, cottage cheese, egg yolks, yogurt, tomato paste, and sugar. Run the machine until all the ingredients are puréed. Remove to a bowl, add salt and pepper to taste.

In a small bowl soak the gelatin in 2 tablespoons cold water. Set the bowl in a saucepan of simmering water and stir the gelatin until it is totally dissolved. Add to the tomato mixture and stir well.

Beat the egg whites with a pinch of salt until stiff. Fold the tomato mixture into the whites and pour the mousse into the mold. Refrigerate for 4 hours.

Dip the mold in hot water for 1 second and turn out onto a round platter. Garnish with sliced tomato and chopped basil.

Yield: 8 servings
Total calories: 530

Chilled Eggs with Tomato Sauce

This dish was served to me one hot summer evening by my friend Edith Ferber, who said that the recipe had been in her family for a *very* long time. It was developed by her grandmother forty years ago when, one night, as the story goes, there was nothing to eat in the house except eggs and tomatoes. Edith has adapted the recipe and added some excellent Virginia ham or boiled ham and her own seasonings.

> 1 tablespoon butter for the mold
> 12 eggs
> salt and pepper
> ¼ pound very good boiled ham, diced
> 1 tablespoon olive oil
> 1 medium onion, chopped
> 3 shallots, chopped
> 2 pounds fresh ripe tomatoes, peeled, quartered, and
>   seeded or a 1-pound can tomatoes, drained
> 1 tablespoon dried thyme
> 1 bay leaf
> 1 teaspoon paprika
> 2 tablespoons yogurt
> 1 bunch watercress for garnish
>
> 5-cup savarin or ring mold

Preheat the oven to 300°.

Butter the mold. Break 6 eggs into the mold, spacing them evenly around the ring. Sprinkle with salt and pepper. Cover the eggs with the diced ham. Then break the remaining 6 eggs on top of the ham. Sprinkle with salt and pepper. Bake at 300° in a *bain-marie* (a pan of hot water) for 30 minutes.

Meanwhile, make the sauce. Heat the oil in a skillet, add the onion and shallots, and cook for 4 minutes over medium heat. Then add the tomatoes, thyme, bay leaf, paprika, and salt and pepper to taste. Cook for 20 minutes, stirring from time to time.

Remove the eggs from the oven and let cool. Unmold the eggs onto a round platter. Add the yogurt to the sauce, mix well, and correct the seasoning. (Remove the bay leaf.) Pour some sauce in the center of the mold and some all around, and refrigerate until ready to serve. Garnish with watercress.

Yield: 8 servings
Total calories: 900

Eggs in Jelly with Shrimp

Eggs in jelly is a very old recipe. It is easy to make, unfattening. Served on a bed of shrimp, it makes a very elegant appetizer or a main course for lunch served with a vegetable salad.

2 envelopes unflavored gelatin
3 tablespoons water + 1 quart
2½ cups chicken bouillon
½ teaspoon soy sauce
salt and pepper
2 tablespoons vinegar
6 eggs
½ pound shrimp, cooked, shelled, and deveined
1½-inch piece fresh ginger, grated
2 tablespoons yogurt
½ tablespoon lime juice
pepper
6 small fresh basil leaves
6 lettuce leaves

6 round ramekins

Make the jelly first. In a small bowl soak the gelatin in 3 tablespoons water. In a saucepan heat the bouillon and then add the gelatin mixture, soy sauce, and salt and pepper to taste. Stir until all the gelatin is dissolved. Set aside to cool.

In a large saucepan bring 1 quart of water to a boil. Reduce the heat to a simmer. Add the vinegar, then gently break the eggs into the simmering water. Cook for 3 to 4 minutes. Carefully remove the eggs with a slotted spoon onto a plate.

In a food processor place the shrimp, ginger, yogurt, lime juice, and some pepper. Run the machine until all the shrimp are chopped fine. Remove to a bowl.

Into each ramekin pour 2 tablespoons jelly and put a basil leaf in the center. Refrigerate until the jelly sets. Trim the eggs. Put them each carefully in a ramekin, smoothest side down, and cover with chopped shrimp. Then add more jelly and refrigerate until ready to serve.

Place 1 lettuce leaf on each plate and unmold an egg on top. Serve with a vegetable salad.

Yield: 6 servings
Total calories: 830

HOT FIRST COURSES & LUNCHEON DISHES

Broiled Frogs' Legs with Coarse Salt

The secret of this dish is small frogs' legs. The big ones are usually tougher and have to be cooked longer. The frogs' legs are marinated in soy sauce and ginger for a couple of hours, then broiled over charcoal and served with coarse salt and chopped scallions. This dish is excellent as an appetizer or as a main course for lunch.

> *8 pairs frogs' legs*
> *4 tablespoons soy sauce*
> *juice of ½ lemon*
> *2-inch piece fresh ginger, minced*
> *salt and pepper*
> *½ cup coarse salt*
> *chopped parsley for garnish*
>
> *charcoal fire*

Wash and pat dry the frogs' legs. Separate the pairs and cut each leg at the joint. Place in a bowl and add the soy sauce, lemon juice, ginger, and some salt and pepper. Toss well and let them marinate for 2 hours.

Broil the frogs' legs over charcoal for 4 minutes on each side. Arrange on a platter with a small bowl of coarse salt in the center. Sprinkle with the chopped parsley and serve.

Yield: 4 servings
Total calories: 275

Sesame Seed and Dill Omelette

This is a good omelette to serve for lunch with some salad, a glass of wine, and a fruit for dessert.

> *6 eggs*
> *2 tablespoons black sesame seeds*
> *½ tablespoon chopped fresh dill*

salt and pepper
1 tablespoon butter
2 tablespoons grated Swiss cheese
1 tablespoon chopped parsley

In a bowl beat the eggs with a fork, then add the sesame seeds, dill, and salt and pepper, and beat lightly again.

In a skillet melt the butter. When it is hot and the foam dies down, add the eggs all at once. They will sizzle. Reduce the heat and cook the eggs, shaking the pan and bringing the edges of the omelette toward the center with a fork. When it is nearly done (very little liquid is left in the center), sprinkle the cheese and chopped parsley in the center. Cook for 1 minute more, then with a spatula fold the omelette in two. Slide it onto a serving platter and serve right away.

Yield: 2 servings
Total calories: 800

Hot Fish Pâté with Dill and Spinach

Many pâtés are wrapped in pastry dough, either to preserve them or to hold them together as they cook. But pastry has a lot of calories. It can be replaced by foil, which is easily removed before serving when the pâté is cold or more carefully removed when it is served hot.

1 pound fresh spinach
salt
1 quart water
½ pound flounder fillets
1 bean curd cake
2 tablespoons flour
pepper
2 tablespoons chopped fresh dill

9-inch pie pan

Wash and trim the spinach and remove the stems. Plunge the spinach into 1 quart of boiling salted water and boil for 3 minutes. Drain immediately, refresh under cold running water, and squeeze most of the water out with your hands.

Place the fish fillets, spinach, bean curd, and flour in the bowl of a food processor. Run the machine until all the ingredients are puréed. Remove to a bowl. Add salt and pepper and the chopped dill. Mix well. Refrigerate for 30 minutes.

Preheat the oven to 450°.

Line the pie pan with foil. Spread the mixture in the pan, cover with another piece of foil, and roll the edges to seal. Make a hole in the center to let steam escape. Bake in the 450° oven for 40 minutes.

Remove the top foil. Place a round platter upside down on top of the pâté and turn it over. Slice and serve hot with a cold tomato salad.

Yield: 4 to 6 servings
Total calories: 430

Salmon Quiche

This quiche is made without any pastry. It is more like a flan than a real quiche. To make serving easier, it is best to use small individual quiche pans. If you make one large quiche in a 9-inch pan, just be careful when serving it.

> *6 eggs*
> *1 cup milk*
> *7 ounces medium-sharp Cheddar, sliced*
> *2 tablespoons chopped chives*
> *2 tablespoons chopped parsley*
> *pepper*
> *1 tablespoon butter, in all*
> *1 large onion, chopped*
> *12 ounces thinly sliced smoked salmon*

Preheat the oven to 550°.

In a large bowl beat together the eggs, milk, cheese, herbs, and pepper. Set aside. In a small skillet melt ½ the butter and sauté the chopped onion over a very low heat until transparent. Add the onion to the egg mixture and mix well.

Butter 4 small quiche pans or 1 large (9-inch) pan with the remaining butter. Pour some of the mixture into the pans or pan. Add ½ the sliced salmon. Pour in the rest of the mixture, then add the remaining sliced salmon.

Bake in the 550° oven for 5 minutes, then lower the heat to 475° and cook for 25 minutes or until the top of the quiche is golden brown. Serve immediately with a green salad or with steamed asparagus.

Yield: 6 servings
Total calories: 2,200

Quiche with Fresh Peas

scant teaspoon butter for the pan
Pâte Brisée (page 233)
1¼ pounds fresh peas in their shells
6 eggs + 1 yolk
6 ounces yogurt
½ cup grated Swiss cheese
1½ tablespoons chopped fresh sage
salt and pepper

Preheat the oven to 400°.

Butter the quiche pan. Roll out the dough and line the pan with it. Prick the bottom with a fork. Bake in the 400° oven for 10 minutes and remove from the oven.

Shell the peas and steam, covered, for 3 minutes until they are barely tender and drain. Beat together the eggs, yogurt, cheese, sage, and salt and pepper.

Place all the peas in the bottom of the quiche shell. Pour the egg mixture over them and bake in the 400° oven for 15 minutes, or until the top is golden brown and a fork inserted in the center comes out clean.

Yield: 6 servings
Total calories: 2,490

Mussel and Spinach Mousse

3 quarts fresh mussels in their shells
2 shallots, chopped
1 cup dry white wine
2 pounds fresh spinach
2 bean curd cakes
1 tablespoon dried tarragon
nutmeg
salt and pepper
juice of 1 lemon

Wash and scrub the mussels. Remove the beards and soak the mussels in cold water for ½ hour, changing the water from time to time. Place the mussels in a large kettle, add the shallots and white wine, cover, and cook over high heat, shaking the pan occasionally until all the shells have opened (about 8 to 10 minutes). Drain the mussels, reserving the liquid. Discard any that have not opened. Remove the mussels from their shells and keep warm.

Wash and trim the spinach and pat dry. Plunge ½ the spinach into boiling water. Drain immediately and refresh under cold running water. Squeeze all the water from the spinach with your hands. Chop the spinach in a food processor and remove to a bowl.

Purée the bean curd in the food processor, fold it into the cooked spinach, and add the tarragon, nutmeg, and salt and pepper.

Cut the remaining raw spinach leaves into narrow strips. Sprinkle with salt, pepper, and lemon juice. Line a large serving bowl with a circle of the raw spinach. In the center place the spinach mousse, then make a "well" in the mousse and in it place the lukewarm mussels.

Sprinkle everything with some of the mussel cooking liquid and serve.

Yield: 4 to 6 servings
Total calories: 1,270

Tomato Stuffed with Fish Mousse

This is an excellent appetizer for the early fall when the tomatoes are large and very ripe.

>   *6 large tomatoes*
>   *½ pound fish fillets (flounder, scrod, etc.)*
>   *3 ounces cottage cheese (1% fat)*
>   *1 egg white*
>   *salt and pepper*
>   *½ tablespoon butter for the pan*
>   *1 tablespoon Madeira*
>   *2 tablespoons chopped chives*

Cut off the tops of the tomatoes and with a spoon remove all the seeds. Place the tomatoes upside down on a paper towel to drain.

In a food processor, place the fish fillets and the cottage cheese and run the machine until they are puréed. Add the white of egg and mix well. Add salt and pepper, run again. Place the fish mixture in the freezer for 1 hour.

Preheat the oven to 450°.

Butter a baking pan. Place the tomatoes in the baking pan side by side. Remove the fish from the freezer, put back in the food processor with the Madeira, and run the machine for ½ minute. Fill the tomatoes with the fish and bake in the 450° oven for 15 minutes. Remove from the oven, sprinkle with the chives, and serve hot.

Yield: 6 servings
Total calories: 510

Hot Crab Mousse

three 4-ounce cans crab meat
5 slices white sandwich bread
½ cup white rum
2 very hot green pimentos
3 garlic cloves
½ pound onions, quartered
salt and pepper
3 egg whites
2 limes for garnish

Drain the crab, pick over for small bones in the meat, and set aside. Soak the bread in the rum.

In a food processor place the crab, hot pimentos, garlic, and onions and run the machine until all the ingredients are chopped very fine. Then add the bread soaked in the rum. Run the machine until all the ingredients are well puréed. Remove to a bowl and season with salt and pepper.

Beat the egg whites until they hold their peaks. Fold them into the crab mixture and transfer the mousse to a serving bowl. Refrigerate for a couple of hours. When ready to serve, garnish with sliced limes.

Yield: 6 to 8 servings
Total calories: 1,260

Mussel Flan with Chervil or Basil Sauce

4 quarts fresh mussels in their shells
2 tablespoons butter, in all
2 shallots, chopped
½ cup dry white wine
6 eggs
8 ounces fish fillet
½ tablespoon cornstarch
salt and pepper
2½ ounces cottage cheese (1% fat)
2½ ounces yogurt
juice of ½ lemon
3 tablespoons chopped fresh chervil or fresh basil

2-quart mold

Scrub and wash the mussels and remove the beards. Place the mussels in a steamer and steam until all the mussels open, (about 8 to 10 minutes). Discard any that have not opened. Remove the mussels from their shells and set aside in a bowl.

In a saucepan melt 1 tablespoon of the butter, add the shallots and the wine, and simmer until the mixture is reduced by half.

In a food processor place the eggs, fish fillets, cornstarch, and the shallot mixture. Run the machine until all the ingredients are puréed.

Butter the mold. Combine the mussels and the egg mixture, correct the seasoning with salt and pepper, and pour into the mold. Cover and seal the mold with foil and steam it, covered, on a rack over 3 cups of boiling water for 25 minutes. Let the flan stand for 5 minutes before unmolding onto a platter.

Make the sauce. Beat the cottage cheese with the yogurt and lemon juice in the processor or with a whisk. Add the chopped chervil or basil, and correct the seasoning with salt and pepper. Heat without boiling and serve from a sauceboat with the flan.

Yield: 6 servings
Total calories: 2,000

Japanese Stock

In the past few years I have become more and more interested in Japanese food for I find it very light, beautiful, and often quite low in calories.

I have been helped by my friend, Madeline Arakawa, who has spent time with me explaining certain ingredients and how to use them. In most American cities you can find Japanese specialty stores or if not, health-food stores, which carry Japanese ingredients. Here is a basic Japanese stock. You can make it ahead of time and freeze it to be used later as a soup base.

1 large piece dried kelp
6 cups water
2 cups shaved dried bonito

Wipe the kelp. Then, with a sharp knife, make several incisions; the flavor of the stock will be better. In a large saucepan place the kelp, cover with the water, and slowly bring to a boil. Just before the water boils, remove the kelp. (If it remains, the stock may be too strong.) When the water boils, lower the heat and add the bonito shavings. Simmer for 1 minute. Turn off the heat. Skim the surface of the stock. Set aside until the shavings have settled at the bottom of the saucepan, then strain through a fine sieve. The stock is ready to use.

Yield: 6 cups
Total calories: 105

Egg Custard with Chives and Tarragon

I first had this custard at a Japanese restaurant. I was quite intrigued for it reminded me of a non-sweet French *crème brûlée.* Then Madeline Arakawa made it for me with different spices from the one I had tasted. This simple dish is very versatile. You can use your imagination and garnish it with mushrooms, mint, shrimp, salmon mousse, anything you may think of.

The custard is so light that it has to be eaten with a spoon. It is excellent for an appetizer or as a main course for lunch.

2½ cups Japanese Stock (page 54)
½ teaspoon salt
1 tablespoon sake
1 teaspoon sugar
1 teaspoon soy sauce
3 eggs
4 teaspoons chopped fresh chives
8 fresh tarragon leaves for garnish

In a saucepan mix the stock with the salt, sake, sugar, and soy sauce. Bring the stock to a boil. Cool.

In a bowl beat the eggs lightly, then beat in the cool stock. Pour the mixture through a fine sieve. Divide the chives among the 4 custard cups and slowly pour in the egg mixture, filling the cups to about ½ inch from the top.

Place the custard cups in a steamer over 3 cups of boiling water. Wrap the lid of the steamer with a dishcloth so that the steam will be absorbed by the cloth and condensation does not fall on the custards. Steam for 15 minutes.

Garnish with 2 tarragon leaves per cup and serve immediately.

Yield: 4 servings
Total calories: 360

NOTE: You can prepare some steamed shrimp and garnish the custards with them; or place a teaspoon of black lumpfish caviar on top of each cup; or, before pouring in the custard, place a raw oyster in the cup.

Eggs in Bean Curd

I wanted to call this dish "Friday Special" because when I was a child I was a boarder in a convent. On Fridays we ate no meat, but on special Fridays we would get individual ramekins with an egg in the center surrounded with either cheese or small pieces of fish. We all loved that dish, as the food usually was rather horrid. I adapted this egg ramekin for an elegant Friday dinner in memory of my convent days.

½ tablespoon butter for the molds
4 soft bean curd cakes
4 eggs
2 tablespoons light soy sauce
salt and pepper
12 asparagus tips (4 inches long)
2 tablespoons red lumpfish caviar
4 tablespoons chopped parsley

4 individual soufflé molds (4 inches in diameter) or small shirred-egg dishes

Preheat the oven to 475°.
   Butter the molds. Place a bean curd cake in each mold. With a soup spoon make a hollow about 3 inches in diameter in the center of each bean curd. Break an egg into each hollow, sprinkle the bean curd with soy sauce, and salt and pepper the eggs. Bake in a *bain-marie* (a pan of hot water) for 10 minutes in the preheated oven.
   Meanwhile, steam the asparagus tips, covered, for 8 minutes over barely simmering water. (Keep the stems to make soup.)
   Remove the molds from the oven. Garnish each with the 4 asparagus tips and place a teaspoon of lumpfish caviar on each egg. Sprinkle with the chopped parsley and serve immediately.

Yield: 4 servings
Total calories: 835

SOUPS

Soft Bean Curd in Iced Consommé

The secret of success for this dish is the quality of the bean curd. It has to be fresh and soft, rather like a custard. The consommé, totally degreased, is served very cold.

>   4 cups beef consommé
>   3 scallions, sliced thin
>   2 soft bean curd cakes
>   1-inch piece fresh ginger, grated

Make the beef consommé with good quality beef bouillon cubes. Refrigerate until ready to serve. Just before serving, add to the consommé the sliced scallions, the bean curd cut into 1-inch cubes, and the grated ginger.

Yield: 4 servings
Total calories: 435

Cold Spinach and Peach Soup

One day walking through Chinatown, I came upon a stand of peaches. They looked superb, the right golden color. I bought 2 pounds on the spot and on my way home bit into one. Horror struck! The peach tasted like mashed potatoes. As I walked home I wondered what I could do with 2 pounds of inedible peaches. This is when I came upon the idea of cooking them to make a cold soup. But if you have good peaches, the fragrance of the soup of course is even better.

>   6 peaches + 1 extra for garnish
>   6 cups chicken stock or bouillon
>   1 pound fresh spinach
>   salt and pepper

Peel and quarter 6 peaches and remove the stones. In a large saucepan bring the bouillon to a boil. Add the peaches and cook for 10 minutes.

Meanwhile, wash and dry the spinach and remove the stems.

Purée the soup and spinach leaves together in a food processor. Pour into a bowl and correct the seasoning. Refrigerate.

To serve, pour into individual bowls and garnish with thin slices of the uncooked peach.

Yield: 6 servings
Total calories: 630

Cold Tomato Soup with Hearts of Palm

My family and I, more precisely my daughter Juliette and I, have a passion for hearts of palm. When I discovered that they were low in calories, we had a field day. For a whole week everything I served had hearts of palm. My husband put a quick stop to it, but one recipe remained—this cold tomato soup made one night for an unexpected guest.

1-pound can stewed tomatoes in heavy tomato purée
juice of 1 lime
2 tablespoons chopped fresh basil leaves
salt and pepper
olive oil
1 or 2 canned hearts of palm, drained
4 small fresh basil leaves for garnish

Place the tomatoes with their purée in a food processor. Add the lime juice, chopped basil, and salt and pepper. Run the machine until all the ingredients are puréed. Correct the seasoning and refrigerate.

Pour the soup into individual bowls and sprinkle each bowl with a few drops of olive oil. Slice the hearts of palm very thin and add 4 or 5 slices to each bowl. Garnish with the basil leaves and serve with wheat crackers.

Yield: 4 servings
Total calories: 455

NOTE: The soup can be heated. Add the sliced hearts of palm just before serving, to heat them through but not to cook.

Cold Spinach and Avocado Soup

1½ pounds fresh spinach
1 slice ripe peeled avocado, 1 inch thick
1-inch piece fresh ginger
3 scallions
½ cup fresh basil leaves
4 cups beef bouillon
1 cup yogurt
salt and pepper

Wash and trim the spinach. Drain in a colander. Cut the avocado slice in pieces. Peel the ginger. Trim the scallions and cut in 2-inch pieces.

Place all the ingredients, except the yogurt, in a food processor. Run the machine for 1 minute, or until all the ingredients are puréed. Remove to a bowl and add the yogurt. Correct the seasoning with salt and pepper.

Refrigerate until ready to serve.

Yield: 4 servings
Total calories: 525

Cold Zucchini-Avocado Soup with Green Grapes

2 medium-size zucchini
1 cup water
5 ounces ripe avocado (about ⅓ of a large avocado)
1 garlic clove
20 fresh mint leaves
16-ounce container yogurt
juice of ½ lime
salt and pepper
small bunch green grapes

Cut the zucchini into 1-inch pieces and place in a saucepan with 1 cup water. Bring to a boil, reduce heat, and simmer until zucchini are just tender. With a slotted spoon remove the zucchini to the bowl of a food processor and add the avocado, garlic, 8 mint leaves, yogurt, and lime juice. Run the machine until all the ingredients are puréed.

Pour the mixture into a bowl, add salt and pepper to taste, and refrigerate until ready to serve. Meanwhile, peel the grapes and set aside (you need 12 grapes in all). To serve, pour the soup into individual bowls, add 3 grapes to each, and garnish with 3 mint leaves.

Yield: 4 servings
Total calories: 620

Cold Lemon-Lima Soup

Marianne, my eldest daughter, is an excellent cook and she watches her diet and mine as a prison guard does a dangerous jail. One night, unexpected guests came for dinner. We had fresh lima beans in the refrigerator and some chopped veal. I was wondering how to make a meal of this when Marianne announced that she would make the soup. She served us this delicious cold lima-bean soup, which is also excellent hot.

1¼ pounds unshelled fresh lima beans or 1 cup shelled
1 cup hot water
zest of 1 lemon
1 teaspoon dried marjoram
½ cup skim milk
1 pint yogurt
salt and a generous amount of pepper
lemon slices for garnish

Shell the lima beans. Steam, covered, for 5 minutes. In a food processor place the lima beans, lemon zest, marjoram, and 3 tablespoons milk. Run the machine until all the ingredients are puréed, then, with the machine still running, add the remaining milk. Pour into a bowl and refrigerate.

When ready to serve, pour the soup into a blender, add the yogurt, and run the machine until the soup is frothy. Add salt and pepper, mix again, and pour into 6 individual bowls. Garnish with lemon slices.

Yield: 6 servings
Total calories: 510

NOTE: To serve hot, heat gently but do not boil.

Tomato and Orange Soup

2 pounds ripe tomatoes
1 onion
1 carrot
4 cups chicken bouillon
juice of 1 orange + the rind
1 bay leaf
salt and pepper
4 small fresh basil leaves for garnish

Peel and seed the tomatoes and chop coarsely. Peel the onion and chop. Cut the carrot into 1-inch pieces.

In a large saucepan, bring the chicken bouillon to a boil and add the tomatoes, orange juice, carrot, onion, bay leaf, and salt and pepper. Bring to a boil again, then reduce the heat and cook over medium heat for 20 minutes or until the carrots are done. Remove the bay leaf.

Purée all the vegetables in a food processor with some of the soup. Pour the purée back into the saucepan and correct the seasoning. Cut the orange rind into a fine julienne and add to soup. Heat and serve garnished with the basil leaves.

Yield: 4 servings
Total calories: 415

NOTE: This soup can be served cold; refrigerate until ready to serve.

Fiddlehead Soup with Snow Peas

A few years ago I was spending a week in the country with my friends the Arakawas. One day, as we were walking in the woods, Arakawa pointed out a fern whose tip was tightly rolled. "They are excellent to eat," he said, "in salad, in soup, as a vegetable." We picked a whole basket of them, brought them home, and under his direction cooked them in four different ways. I later learned that these ferns were fiddleheads, young shoots of an ostrich fern, which grows in the north and is a great delicacy in Canada. Now fiddleheads can be found in supermarkets and vegetable stores in the spring.

To prepare fiddleheads: Shake the fiddleheads in a wire basket to remove their light brown coating. Snap off about 1 inch of the stems. Soak in cold water to remove any grit. Pat dry in paper towels. They can now be stored for a week in the refrigerator or frozen for later use.

½ pound fiddleheads
¼ pound fresh snow peas
6 cups bouillon or Japanese Stock (page 54)
salt and pepper
juice of 1 lime
2 tablespoons chopped fresh basil leaves for garnish

Wash and prepare the fiddleheads as described above. Set 6 aside for garnish. Wash and trim the snow peas. Set aside.

In a large saucepan, bring the stock to a boil. Add the fiddleheads, reduce the heat, and cook for 10 minutes.

Purée the soup in a blender or a food processor. Pour back into the saucepan and add the snow peas and the 6 reserved fiddleheads. Cook for 2 minutes. Turn off the heat. Correct seasoning by adding salt, pepper, and some lime juice to taste.

Serve in individual bowls, sprinkled with the chopped basil.

Yield: 6 servings
Total calories: 230

Artichoke Soup with Lemon Grass

Walking one day through Chinatown, I came across a small vegetable stand that sold something that looked like scallions but were very hard and had a dark yellow bulb. I asked what it was, but to no avail, as the woman did not speak a word of English. This is something that often happens to me, but I have devised a strategy: First I buy whatever is new and unknown to me, then I wait around. Somebody is bound to come along who speaks some English and is willing to help. Sometimes the merchant starts to feel sorry for me and calls in Chinese to a young boy in the street to go find someone who will translate. It worked that time, and soon I was surrounded with people telling me that these were not scallions but lemon grass, which could be used in the same way as fresh ginger; that it was excellent for your health, good in soup, salads, etc.

This recipe is the first one in which I experimented with lemon grass. It is now found in fancy specialty stores and soon will be available everywhere in the United States. It has a marvelous fragrance—a mixture of lemon and scallion.

> *12-ounce can artichoke bottoms*
> *3 lemon grass stalks*
> *6 cups Japanese Stock or bouillon (page 54)*
> *salt and pepper*
> *chopped parsley or watercress for garnish*

Drain the artichokes. Wash and trim the lemon grass. Cut in 1-inch pieces. Purée the artichokes and the lemon grass in a food processor with 1 cup of stock. Strain through a sieve.

Pour the mixture into a saucepan and add the remaining stock. Add salt and pepper to taste. Slowly bring to a boil. Pour the soup into individual bowls, garnish with parsley or watercress, and serve.

Yield: 6 servings
Total calories: 185

Fennel Soup

2 fennel bulbs
4 cups chicken bouillon
salt and pepper
2 tablespoons chopped parsley for garnish

Snip off with scissors some of the feathery leaves of the fennel to use for garnish. Cut ½ inch off the tops of the bulbs, and also cut 4 thin slices for garnish. Cut the rest of the fennel bulbs into julienne strips.

In a large saucepan bring the chicken bouillon to a boil; add the julienne of fennel and cook for 10 minutes. Purée the soup in a blender or a food processor. Pour the soup back into the saucepan and correct the seasoning.

In each serving bowl place a slice of fennel, pour the hot soup over it, sprinkle with snipped fennel leaves and some chopped parsley, and serve immediately.

Yield: 4 servings
Total calories: 135

Endive Soup

6 endives
1 teaspoon sugar
6 cups chicken bouillon
1 tablespoon lemon juice
salt and pepper
½ cup chopped parsley for garnish

Wash and slice the endives. In a saucepan, place the endives, sprinkle with the sugar, then add ½ cup of the chicken bouillon. Cook over high heat for 5 minutes until the endives are lightly browned and the bouillon has evaporated. Then add the remaining bouillon and the lemon juice, salt, and pepper and cook for 15 minutes. Pour the soup into a blender and purée. Pour back into the saucepan and correct the seasoning.

Reheat. Pour into individual soup bowls, and divide the parsley among the bowls. Serve right away.

Yield: 6 servings
Total calories: 140

Cucumber and Spinach Soup

1 bunch fresh spinach (about ½ pound)
1 large cucumber
1 garlic clove
6 cups chicken bouillon
1 tablespoon dried sage
salt and pepper

Wash and pat dry the spinach. Remove the stems. Peel the cucumber. Cut in two lengthwise and remove the seeds. Cut in 2-inch pieces.

Purée the cucumber, garlic, and spinach in a food processor or a blender with 2 cups of the stock.

Pour the soup into a saucepan, add the remaining stock, heat, and add the sage. Correct the seasoning with salt and pepper. Serve piping hot.

Yield: 6 servings
Total calories: 135

Gai Lohn (Chinese Kale) Soup with Lettuce

Chinese kale is found today in numerous supermarkets and vegetable stores. Its taste is similar to mustard greens, but more
subtle. Mixed with lettuce, it is an ideal vegetable for making
soup.

1 pound Chinese kale
1 head Boston lettuce
6 cups chicken bouillon
2 tablespoons milk
salt and pepper
4 slices day-old Italian bread
1 garlic clove, chopped and crushed

Wash the kale, cut off the stems, and cut the leaves into strips.
Wash the Boston lettuce and cut the leaves into strips. Put the
kale and lettuce in a large saucepan, cover with the bouillon, and
bring to a boil. Reduce heat and simmer for 10 minutes.

Purée the cooked greens in a blender with 1 cup of the broth.
Pour the purée back into the saucepan, add the milk, and correct
the seasoning with salt and pepper. Toast the bread and spread
the crushed garlic on the toast. Reheat the soup. Place 1 piece of
toast in each soup bowl, pour in the soup, and serve.

Yield: 4 servings
Total calories: 390

String-Bean Soup with Hard-Boiled Eggs

½ pound string beans
4 cups chicken bouillon
½ cup cream of wheat
salt and pepper
1 teaspoon dried thyme
3 hard-boiled eggs (yolks only)

Trim the string beans and cut on the bias into 1-inch pieces. Wash and drain. In a saucepan bring the chicken bouillon to a boil, add the string beans, and cook for 10 minutes or until tender.

Put the cream of wheat in a bowl and mix with 3 tablespoons of the hot bouillon. Add the cream of wheat to the soup and cook, simmering, for 5 minutes. Add salt and pepper and the thyme.

Pour the soup into 4 individual bowls. Squeeze the egg yolks through a fine sieve on top of each serving. Serve immediately.

Yield: 4 servings
Total calories: 575

Asparagus Soup with Black Lumpfish Caviar

1 pound asparagus
4 cups chicken bouillon
10 small fresh basil leaves
2 egg yolks
4 tablespoons yogurt
salt and pepper
2-ounce jar black lumpfish caviar

Wash and trim the asparagus and cut into 1-inch pieces. In a large saucepan put the chicken bouillon, add the asparagus, and cook for 10 minutes or until it is tender. In a blender purée the asparagus with the bouillon and 6 of the basil leaves.

Pour the soup back into the saucepan. Beat together the egg yolks and yogurt, add to the soup, and mix with a wooden spoon. Season with salt and pepper and heat gently. Pour the soup into 4 individual bowls, add 1 rounded teaspoon of lumpfish caviar to each bowl, and garnish with the remaining basil leaves.

Yield: 4 servings
Total calories: 395

Cabbage Soup

2½- to 3-pound crinkly-leafed Savoy cabbage
2 beef bouillon cubes
2 quarts water
¼ teaspoon hot red pepper sauce
1 garlic clove, finely minced
1 pound mushrooms
salt and pepper

Cut the cabbage in four and remove the center core. In a large soup kettle, dissolve the 2 bouillon cubes in 2 quarts of water. Add the cabbage, bring to a boil, and lower the heat. Simmer for 10 minutes.

With a slotted spoon remove the cabbage to the bowl of a food processor. Chop the cabbage and return it to the soup. Add the hot sauce and minced garlic.

Wash the mushrooms, pat dry, and remove the stems. Slice the caps and add to the soup. Cook for 5 minutes. Correct the seasoning and serve piping hot.

Yield: 6 servings
Total calories: 445

Sorrel and Beet Soup

Sorrel, which is often called sour grass in the United States because of its bitter taste, is marvelous to use in soups and sauces. The leaves—small, smooth, and dark green—have a long stem. Sorrel has to be well washed for the leaves are often full of sand.

   1 pound sorrel
   1-pound can beets
   1 tablespoon butter
   1 tablespoon flour
   6 cups chicken bouillon
   2 tablespoons chopped fresh chives
   salt and pepper

Wash and trim the sorrel, removing all the stems. Pat dry. Drain the beets. In a food processor, with a julienne shredding blade, shred the beets. (You can also do this with a sharp knife.) Set aside.

   In a skillet, melt the butter. When it is hot, add the sorrel, sauté for 2 or 3 minutes, then add the flour. Mix well and cook for 2 minutes more. Transfer the sorrel to the food processor and purée.

   Heat the chicken bouillon with the chives. Add the puréed sorrel and the julienne of beets, and mix well. Correct the seasoning, heat through, and serve.

Yield: 4 to 5 servings
Total calories: 435

Sauerkraut Soup

3 potatoes
2 onions
1 tablespoon butter
1 tablespoon flour
6 cups chicken stock or bouillon
¾ pound sauerkraut
salt and pepper
chopped parsley for garnish

Peel the potatoes and slice thin. Place in a bowl of cold water. Peel the onions and chop fine.

In a large saucepan melt the butter, add the chopped onions, and brown for a few minutes. Sprinkle the onions with flour, mix well, then slowly add the bouillon, stirring with a wooden spoon. Drain the potatoes, add them to the soup, and simmer for 15 minutes.

Meanwhile, wash and drain the sauerkraut. When the potatoes are nearly done, add the sauerkraut to the soup. Correct the seasoning, and cook for 10 minutes more. Serve garnished with chopped parsley.

Yield: 4 servings
Total calories: 705

Split Pea Soup with Sorrel Purée

Sorrel is available in the spring. Cooked and puréed, it will keep very well frozen. To freeze, just parboil the washed sorrel, do not cook. Drain, squeeze the water out, and purée. Store in plastic containers in the freezer.

3 medium potatoes
3 leeks
2 onions
½ pound split peas
2 quarts water or chicken bouillon
1 bay leaf
salt and pepper
½ cup sorrel purée

Peel the potatoes and cut in very small dice. Wash the leeks and slice thin. Peel and chop the onions.

Place the split peas in a large kettle and add the water or bouillon. Bring to a boil, reduce the heat, and simmer, covered, for 1 hour. Then add the vegetables, bay leaf, and salt and pepper, and simmer until all the vegetables are cooked. Add the sorrel purée, mix well, correct the seasoning, and serve.

Yield: 6 servings
Total calories: 1,430

Onion Soup with Goat Cheese

When I was living in Dodoma, Tanzania, many foods were difficult to find. Cheese was a mystery of nature, meat was too tough to eat, and butter and bread were but a dream. But there were onions, beans, and goat's milk. The onions were sold in the market in piles of three, the beans by cups, and the goat's milk by the gallon. Having bought goat's milk and found out that no one in my family would drink it, I decided to make cheese. An Australian friend taught me how. You have to boil the milk and add lime juice (limes were plentiful). The milk will curdle. Then it is put in a fine sieve overnight to drain, and the next day you have cheese. I did it—I made cheese and then, with my onions, made a great soup. We ate it for three days. However, this recipe makes enough for only one dinner for 6 guests.

6 large onions
1 tablespoon butter
salt and pepper
4 cups chicken bouillon
1 tablespoon cornstarch
1 cup dry white wine
6 biscottes (or Holland rusks)
¼ pound goat cheese (the soft kind)
chopped parsley for garnish

Peel and slice the onions. In a skillet, melt the butter, add the onions, and sauté over a very high heat for 5 minutes. Add salt and pepper to taste.

In a large saucepan heat the bouillon. Add the onions and simmer for 10 minutes. Correct the seasoning. Mix the cornstarch with the white wine. Add to the soup and cook for another 5 minutes.

Place a *biscotte* in each soup bowl. Slice the goat cheese and put a couple of slices on each *biscotte*. Pour in the soup, garnish with parsley, and serve.

Yield: 6 servings
Total calories: 1,090

Escarole Soup with Eggs

This is a quick soup to make at the end of a busy day on a cold winter evening. In this recipe, I used escarole as a base; you can make the soup with many other vegetables, such as spinach, celery, or string beans.

1 small head escarole
3 garlic cloves
1 tablespoon olive oil
4 cups chicken bouillon
salt and pepper
4 eggs
4 slices day-old Italian bread
2 tablespoons chopped parsley

Wash the escarole and drain. With a sharp knife cut the leaves into 3-inch pieces. Peel and chop the garlic.

In a large saucepan heat the olive oil and add the garlic. Sauté for 3 minutes, then add the escarole, bouillon and salt and pepper. Simmer for 15 minutes.

While the soup is simmering, carefully break the eggs into it, poach them for 4 minutes, then remove with a slotted spoon onto a plate. Sprinkle with pepper and chopped parsley and keep warm.

Toast the bread, place a slice in each serving bowl, and then pour in the soup. Slide an egg onto each piece of toast and serve.

Yield: 4 servings
Total calories: 665

Mushroom Soup with Clams

> 6 large hard-shell clams
> ½ pound mushrooms
> 2 cups bottled clam juice
> 2 cups chicken bouillon
> salt and pepper
> parsley for garnish
> 1 lime for garnish

Wash and scrub the clams and soak for 1 hour in cold water. Wash, pat dry, and quarter the mushrooms.

In a food processor or a blender, purée the mushrooms with 1 cup of the clam juice. Pour the purée into a saucepan, add the remaining clam juice and the chicken bouillon, and bring to a boil. Simmer for 5 minutes.

In another saucepan place the drained clams, cover, and cook over high heat until they open (about 8 minutes). Remove the clams and discard any that have not opened. Drain the liquid through a fine sieve and add to the mushroom soup. Correct the seasoning. Pour the soup into 6 bowls and place an open clam in each bowl. Garnish with a parsley sprig and a thin slice of lime.

Yield: 6 servings
Total calories: 285

Edith's Curry Scallop Soup

I write no cookbook without my friend Edith's contribution. She is not only one of the best cooks in New York, but she excels in low-calorie cooking. On one of my trips to Africa, I brought her back cloves from Zanzibar. She developed this recipe, tried it on many friends, then allowed me to use it. This soup served at lunch is a meal in itself. If you serve it for dinner, follow it with something light, such as an omelette and a salad, with a simple fruit for dessert.

1 pound tomatoes
1 pound sea scallops
2 quarts chicken bouillon
1 tablespoon curry powder
1 tablespoon dried thyme
1-inch piece fresh ginger, grated
3 cloves
salt and pepper
2 tablespoons chopped parsley for garnish

Dip the tomatoes in boiling water and peel them. Quarter, remove all the seeds, and chop fine. Set aside. Wash and pat dry the sea scallops. Cut into bite-size pieces. Set aside.

Heat the bouillon, add the curry powder, thyme, grated ginger, and cloves. Cook for 5 minutes. Then add the tomatoes and the scallops. Correct the seasoning and simmer for 5 minutes. Serve piping hot, garnished with the chopped parsley.

Yield: 8 servings
Total calories: 660

Mussel and Sorrel Soup

1 quart fresh mussels in their shells
2 garlic cloves, chopped
¼ cup chopped parsley
pepper
4 cups Japanese Stock (page 54)
2 pounds sorrel
1 tablespoon sugar (optional)
salt (optional)

Wash and scrub the mussels, remove the beards, and soak the mussels for ½ hour in cold water, changing the water several times.

In a large kettle place the mussels, chopped garlic, and parsley. Add pepper and ¼ cup of the stock. Cook over medium heat until the mussels are open (about 8 to 10 minutes). With a slotted spoon remove the mussels to a bowl to cool. Discard any that have not opened. Strain the mussel cooking juices through a very fine sieve. In a saucepan combine the cooking juices and the Japanese Stock.

Wash the sorrel carefully. Drain. Place the sorrel in a food processor with ½ cup of the soup. Purée the sorrel, and add it to the soup. Correct the seasoning, adding salt and sugar, if necessary. Cook for 5 minutes.

Remove the mussels from their shells and add to the soup. Reheat briefly and serve.

Yield: 4 servings
Total calories: 575

Consommé with Mung Bean Noodles and Veal Meatballs

Mung bean noodles are Chinese but can be found in many super-markets. They are sold dried in 2-, 4-, or 7-ounce skeins. They are white in color. To use, first soak them in hot water until they are rubbery. Then they can be cooked. The noodles should be cut with scissors into manageable lengths.

¾ pound chopped veal
1 egg
2 tablespoons bread crumbs
1-inch piece fresh ginger, grated
few drops sesame oil
salt and pepper
4 ounces mung bean noodles
6 cups chicken consommé or bouillon
2 tablespoons chopped parsley for garnish
grated Parmesan

In a bowl, mix together the veal, egg, bread crumbs, ginger, and sesame oil. Add salt and pepper to taste. Mix well and form into small balls the size of a walnut.

Place the mung bean noodles in a large bowl and cover with boiling water. Let soak until rubbery, then drain and set aside.

Heat the consommé or bouillon. When it boils, add the meat-balls and simmer for 5 minutes. Then add the noodles and cook for 5 minutes more. Divide the soup and meatballs among 6 individual bowls, sprinkle with parsley, and serve with grated Parmesan on the side.

Yield: 6 servings
Total calories: 1,235

Soupe de Poissons d'Été

This is a main-dish soup.

> 3 pounds fish, cut in serving pieces (such as flounder, tile
>   fish, mackerel, halibut, sea bass—some of each;
>   see Note)
> 1 large onion
> 2 large ripe tomatoes
> 1 leek
> 2 carrots
> 3 large garlic cloves
> 1 fennel bulb
> 4 cups vegetable or chicken bouillon
> salt and pepper
> 2 tablespoons dried thyme
> 1 bay leaf
> zest of ½ orange, cut into fine julienne strips
> 3 egg yolks
> lemon juice
> 1 tablespoon strong olive oil
> 6 slices day-old Italian bread, toasted
> 2 tablespoons chopped parsley for garnish

Wash and pat dry the fish. Peel and chop the onion. Peel, quarter, and seed the tomatoes, then chop coarsely. Wash and trim the leek and slice thin. Slice the carrots thin. Peel and chop the garlic. Wash and cut the fennel into thin slices.

In a large casserole place all the vegetables. Add 2 cups of the bouillon, salt and pepper, and the thyme, bay leaf, and orange zest. Bring to a boil, then reduce the heat and simmer for 10 minutes.

Add the fish and cook for another 10 minutes (see Note). When the fish is cooked, remove it with a spatula to a large soup bowl.

Beat together the egg yolks and 3 tablespoons of bouillon and add to the vegetables, stirring. Add some lemon juice, the olive oil, and the remaining bouillon. Simmer the soup for 5 more minutes and pour it over the fish.

Place the toasted bread on top, sprinkle with chopped parsley, and serve.

Yield: 6 servings
Total calories: 2,195

NOTE: After serving this soup several times, I found that some people are afraid of fish bones in soup. If this is the case for you, use fish fillets, but cook the fish for only 5 minutes.

Chorba

This is an Arab soup. It is a meal in itself, and you should just serve a salad and fruit after it.

1 large onion
3 carrots
3 zucchini
4 potatoes
4 small turnips
2 leeks
2 pounds tomatoes
1 pound beef (bottom round or round)
1 tablespoon olive oil
2 quarts water
2 sprigs coriander (Chinese parsley)
1 teaspoon dried mint
1 teaspoon cumin
salt and pepper

Peel the onion and chop. Cut the carrots in small dice. Wash the zucchini and dice. Peel, wash, and dice the potatoes. Peel, wash, and dice the turnips. Wash and slice the leeks. Peel, quarter, and seed the tomatoes, and dice. Cut the meat in small dice.

In a large soup kettle, heat the olive oil. Add the onion and cook over a low flame for 10 minutes, stirring with a wooden spoon. Add the beef and brown on all sides.

Add 2 quarts of water, bring to a boil, and skim the top several times. Then reduce the heat and add all the vegetables and spices. Cook for 45 minutes.

Correct the seasoning. Serve piping hot.

Yield: 4 servings
Total calories: 2,200

FISH & SHELLFISH

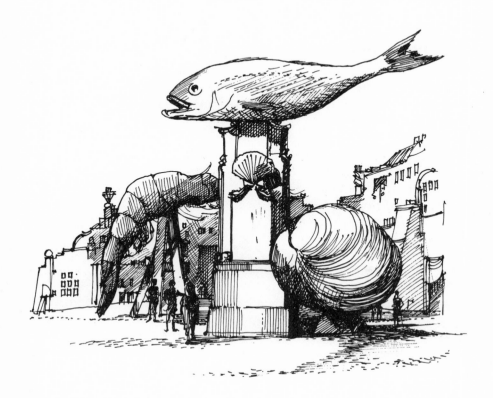

Steamed Fillet of Flounder in Lettuce Leaves

The most important ingredient in this recipe is the fish. The fillets have to be very thin because when they are stuffed and rolled they must cook evenly.

> 3 fillets of flounder (about 1 pound)
> 1 large head iceberg lettuce (see Note)
> 1 pound Swiss chard
> salt and pepper
> 1 tablespoon dried sage
> 1 pint yogurt
> 2 lemons
> 4 fresh mint leaves, chopped

Rinse the fillets under cold water, pat dry, and cut in half crosswise. Blanch the head of iceberg lettuce (put it in hot water for 2 minutes), then refresh immediately under cold running water and drain. This will help to separate the leaves easily. Peel off 6 large leaves.

Wash and pat dry the Swiss chard. Steam it, covered, for 3 minutes. Drain and squeeze to remove all the water. Chop the Swiss chard and sprinkle lightly with salt and pepper.

On each lettuce leaf, place ½ a fish fillet. Lightly sprinkle with salt and pepper and the sage. Cover with chopped chard and roll up the fish in the lettuce leaf. Place the rolled fillets in a circle in a steamer. Steam, covered, for 15 minutes.

Mix the yogurt with the juice of ½ lemon, add salt and pepper to taste, and add the mint. Serve the fish on a platter with lemon slices and serve the yogurt sauce on the side.

Yield: 3 servings
Total calories: 715

NOTE: You may need 2 heads of iceberg lettuce if 1 head does not provide enough perfect large leaves.

Baked Fillet of Sole with Lime

8 fillets of sole (about 2 pounds)
2 large limes
salt and pepper
2 tablespoons butter
16 green olives, pitted
chopped parsley for garnish

Wash and pat dry the sole fillets and place in a baking dish. Use a baking dish from which you can serve the fish. Squeeze the limes and pour the juice over the fillets. Refrigerate overnight.

The next day, preheat the oven to 375°. Sprinkle the fish with salt and pepper. Cut the butter into small pieces and sprinkle over the fish. Bake the fish for 15 minutes, then add the green olives, and bake for another 5 minutes. Serve immediately, sprinkled with chopped parsley.

Yield: 4 servings
Total calories: 1,025

Broiled Fillet of Flounder Stuffed with Broccoli

8 fillets of flounder (about 2 pounds)
1 bunch broccoli
salt and pepper
½ tablespoon dried sage
1 teaspoon sesame oil
2 tablespoons capers
1 egg
3 tablespoons yogurt
1 cup fine bread crumbs
2 lemons for garnish
1 tablespoon vegetable oil

wooden toothpicks

Wash and pat dry the fish fillets. Cut the core and stems off the broccoli. Steam the broccoli florets, covered, for 5 minutes. Remove to a bowl. Sprinkle with salt, pepper, and sage, add the sesame oil, and mix well. Place some broccoli in the center of each fish fillet, add a couple of capers, and roll up. Secure with toothpicks.

In a bowl, beat together the egg and the yogurt. Roll each fillet in the egg mixture, then in bread crumbs, pressing on the bread crumbs with your fingers. Brush each roll with a little oil so the bread crumbs will not burn.

Broil under a hot broiler for 10 minutes on each side. Remove to a serving platter, sprinkle with the remaining capers, and garnish with lemon wedges.

Yield: 4 servings
Total calories: 1,315

Turban of Sole with Smoked Salmon

2 tablespoons butter for the mold
8 slices smoked salmon (about ½ pound)
12 small fillets of sole (about 2 pounds)
4 eggs, separated

1 cup yogurt
½ cup shelled pistachio nuts
salt and pepper
watercress
lemons for garnish
Parsley Sauce (page 224)

4-cup savarin *or ring mold*

Preheat the oven to 325°.

Butter the mold. Line the mold with the slices of salmon, alternating with 8 of the sole fillets. Half of each piece of fish should hang over the edge of the mold.

In a food processor place the remaining 4 sole fillets, the egg yolks, yogurt, and pistachio nuts. Run the machine until all the ingredients are puréed. Remove to a bowl and correct the seasoning with salt and pepper.

Beat the egg whites stiff. Fold the fish mixture into the egg whites and pour the mousse into the mold. Fold the salmon and the fish fillets over the mousse. Cover with foil and bake in a *bain-marie* (a pan of hot water) in the 325° oven for 45 minutes.

Line a round platter with the watercress. Unmold the fish on a cake rack so as to discard any cooking liquid. Slide it onto the watercress and serve with lemon wedges and Parsley Sauce.

Yield: 6 servings
Total calories: 2,595

Baked Striped Bass on a Bed of Seaweed

I thought of this recipe one summer evening after a trip to Montauk Point. We had gone to the piers to see the fishing boats come in. One boat was full of striped bass. I bought a 5-pound striper because it had seaweed around its jaws; it seemed to be sleeping on the seaweed. For this dish I now use Japanese seaweed, which can be found in most Oriental markets or a well-supplied health-food store. When cooked, it is soft and transparent but still dark green.

> 1 ounce Ito Wakame (Japanese seaweed; see page 113)
> 5-pound striped bass (see Note)
> 10 peppercorns
> 1 bay leaf
> 1 onion stuck with a clove
> 1 carrot, sliced
> 1 quart water
> 3 lemons
> salt and pepper
> 1 bunch parsley
> 2-inch piece fresh ginger, peeled and sliced thin
> 2 tablespoons soy sauce
> 1 cup dry white wine
> Soy Sauce with Japanese Horseradish (page 220)

Preheat the oven to 375°.

Soak the seaweed in a bowl of cold water. Cut off the head and tail of the striped bass, place them in a large saucepan and add the peppercorns, bay leaf, onion, and sliced carrot. Cover with 1 quart of water, bring to a boil, then reduce the heat to medium, and cook for 20 minutes.

Meanwhile, wash and pat dry the fish. Make 2 diagonal slits on both sides of the fish and rub it with the juice of 1 of the lemons. Sprinkle with salt and pepper, inside and out. Wash the parsley and chop coarsely. Fill the fish's cavity with the parsley. Place the sliced ginger inside the slits.

Drain the seaweed. Line a baking pan with the seaweed, place the fish on top, and rub the top of the fish with the soy sauce. Pour over it 1 cup of the fish stock and the wine. Bake in the 375°

oven for 30 minutes. Then add 1 more cup of fish stock and baste the fish. Cook for another 30 minutes, basting from time to time. The fish is cooked when it flakes easily when tested with a fork.

Serve the fish on a large platter, surrounded by the seaweed. Cut the remaining lemons into quarters and garnish the fish. On the side serve the Soy Sauce with Japanese Horseradish.

Yield: 6 servings
Total calories: 1,305

NOTE: If you buy the striped bass in a fish store, ask the fishmonger to cut off the head and tail and remove the center bone. Head and tail plus the bone will make an excellent fish stock and guests love to eat a fish with no bones.

Braised Striped Bass with Cider

My mother made this recipe for me when I went back to France for a visit. The French cider has an alcohol content of about 12.2 percent and about 75 calories in 6 ounces.

2 heads Boston lettuce
½ tablespoon butter for baking dish
4 striped bass fillets (about 2 pounds)
pepper
8 very thin slices prosciutto
6 ounces sparkling French apple cider
2 lemons, sliced, for garnish

Preheat the oven to 450°.

Wash the lettuce and pat dry. Butter a shallow ovenproof baking dish. (Use a baking dish from which you can serve the fish.) Line the dish with the large leaves of the lettuce.

Wash and pat dry the fish and sprinkle with pepper. Place the fish on top of the lettuce, skin side down. Cover with the prosciutto, then with more lettuce leaves. Sprinkle the lettuce with pepper, and pour the cider over all.

Cover the pan with foil and bake in the 450° oven for 20 minutes. Then reduce the heat to 375°, uncover the fish, baste with the pan juices, and cook for another 15 minutes. Test with a fork to see if it flakes easily. Serve the fish surrounded with lemon slices.

Yield: 6 servings
Total calories: 1,240

Steamed Cod with Fresh Basil and Ginger

For years the word "cod" sent shivers down my back, reminding me of my childhood years spent in a boarding school where some gray type of fish, "cod" by name, was served to us. Only when I came to the United States and traveled through New England did I discover not only that fresh cod is delicious, but also that it has very few calories. Marvelous things can be accomplished with cod. One of them is by steaming, with the fish wrapped in foil to keep its juices and served with a yogurt sauce or just with lemon.

4 cod steaks, about 1 inch thick (2 pounds)
2 scallions, cut in 1-inch pieces
1-inch piece fresh ginger, peeled and sliced
2 tablespoons chopped fresh basil leaves
2 tablespoons mushroom soy sauce
salt and pepper
parsley for garnish
2 lemons, sliced, for garnish

Wash and pat dry the cod steaks. Cut 4 pieces of foil each big enough to hold a piece of the fish. Place the cod in the center of the foil, and on top of each piece put some cut-up scallions, 1 or 2 slices of ginger, and ½ tablespoon of basil. Sprinkle with soy sauce, salt (very little), and pepper. Close the foil tightly around each slice.

Place the fish in a steamer and steam, covered, for 10 minutes. Carefully remove the fish from the foil. Arrange on a serving platter and garnish with parsley and lemon slices.

Yield: 4 servings
Total calories: 820

Baked Cod with Clams and Carrots

4 cod steaks, about 1 inch thick (2 pounds)
2 pounds hard-shell clams
1 onion, chopped
1 pound carrots, sliced thin
pepper
2 teaspoons chopped fresh thyme
1 lime, sliced, for garnish

Wash and pat dry the cod steaks. Scrape and wash the clams and soak for 1 hour in cold water. Place the drained clams in a large kettle, cover, and cook over high heat until they open (about 6 to 8 minutes). Discard any that do not open. Drain the clams. Reserve the juice and strain it. When the clams are cool to the touch, remove from the shells.

Preheat the oven to 475°.

Line a baking pan with the chopped onion and sliced carrots, add the clam juice, and sprinkle with pepper and some of the thyme. Place the fish steaks on top. Sprinkle with more pepper and the remaining thyme.

Bake in the 475° oven for 15 minutes. Add the clams to the baking pan and cook for another 5 minutes. Serve garnished with sliced lime.

Yield: 4 servings
Total calories: 1,240

Tilefish en Papillote with Sorrel Sauce

4 slices tilefish, about 2 inches thick (2 pounds)
salt and pepper
2 tablespoons capers
2 pounds sorrel
½ cup yogurt
1 teaspoon butter
½ teaspoon sugar (optional)
2 limes, sliced, for garnish

foil paper

Preheat the oven to 425°.

Wash and pat dry the fish. Cut 4 pieces of foil, each big enough to wrap a piece of the fish (about 8 by 8 inches). Place the fish in the center of the foil and sprinkle with salt and pepper and capers. Wrap the fish, place in a baking pan, and bake in the 425° oven for 20 minutes.

Meanwhile, wash and trim the sorrel. Steam it, covered, for 3 minutes. Remove to a chopping board and chop coarsely with a knife. Put the sorrel in a saucepan, add the yogurt, salt and pepper to taste, and the butter. Add the sugar *if* the sorrel is bitter. Mix well and heat. Do not let the sauce boil.

Remove the fish from the oven and arrange on a platter. Spoon the sauce over it and serve with sliced lime.

Yield: 4 servings
Total calories: 1,035

Braised Halibut

15 sorrel leaves or Swiss chard
2 pounds halibut fillets
2 tablespoons butter
10 mint leaves
6 parsley sprigs
salt and pepper
juice of 1 lemon
6 tablespoons yogurt

Remove the stems from the sorrel or Swiss chard and wash and pat the leaves dry. Wash and pat dry the halibut.

In a large saucepan, melt the butter, add the sorrel or Swiss chard, and cook over medium heat for 5 minutes. Place the fish fillets on top, and add the mint, parsley sprigs, and salt and pepper. Cover and cook over low heat for 20 minutes or more, depending on how thick the fillets are.

Remove the fish from the saucepan to a serving platter. Add the lemon juice to the saucepan, heat, then pour the greens and liquid into a food processor and purée. Add the yogurt, correct the seasoning, and pour the sauce over the fish.

Serve with plain cooked *orzo* (small rice-shaped pasta) or a steamed vegetable.

Yield: 4 servings
Total calories: 1,200

Broiled Halibut Steak

4 halibut steaks, about 2 inches thick (2 pounds)
2 tablespoons light soy sauce
juice of 1 lime
1-inch piece fresh ginger, grated
1 tablespoon dried oregano
1 tablespoon oil
4 scallions, sliced
2 lemons, cut into wedges, for garnish
4 large ripe tomatoes, halved and seasoned with salt, pepper,
    and oregano

Wash and pat dry the steaks. In a bowl mix together the soy sauce, lime juice, grated ginger, and oregano. Add the halibut steaks and marinate for 2 hours.

Preheat the broiler.

Remove the steaks from the marinade, brush with oil, and broil 4 inches from the heat for 5 minutes on each side. Check if the steaks are done by pushing the flesh in the center near the bone with a fork. It should feel just barely firm. When the fish is done, remove to a platter.

Heat the marinade in a small saucepan, add the scallions, and pour over the fish. Garnish with lemon wedges and serve with the tomatoes "broiled" in the oven for 20 to 30 minutes. (Start them before you broil the fish.)

Yield: 4 servings
Total calories: 1,160

Broiled Red Snapper with Dill Sauce

2 whole red snappers, about 2 pounds each
salt and pepper
1 soft bean curd cake
2 tablespoons snipped fresh dill
1 lemon, sliced, for garnish

Preheat the broiler.
   Wash and pat dry the snappers. Crosswise, make 2 slits in the skin of each fish. Sprinkle inside and out with salt and pepper.
   In a food processor place the bean curd and the dill. Run the machine until the bean curd is puréed and the dill is chopped fine. Add salt and pepper.
   Broil the fish 8 to 10 inches from the heat, 5 minutes on each side. Garnish with the sliced lemon and serve with the dill sauce.

Yield: 4 servings
Total calories: 1,040

Red Snapper with Cucumbers

1 red snapper, filleted (about 2 pounds)
juice of 2 limes
1 large cucumber
1 tablespoon coarse salt
½ cup yogurt
1 teaspoon strong Dijon mustard
3 tablespoons chopped fresh chives
salt and pepper

Wash the cucumber and slice very thin. Sprinkle with coarse salt and set aside on a plate so that the cucumber sweats its water. Drain before using.
   Wash the red snapper fillets and pat dry. Place them in a steamer and steam, covered, for 5 minutes until barely done. Remove carefully to a platter, pour the lime juice over them, and set aside.

In a bowl, mix together the yogurt, mustard, and 2 table-spoons of the chives. Add salt and pepper to taste. Mix well.

Arrange the fish fillets on a platter, cover with the sauce, and surround with cucumber slices. Sprinkle with the remaining chives and serve at room temperature.

Yield: 4 servings
Total calories: 985

Poached Cold Red Snapper with Watercress Sauce

The design of this dish is to serve a dozen small fish arranged like the rays of the sun around a mound of sliced carrots and onions topped with a layer of seaweed. The fish is served cold (the court-bouillon, when cold, will be jellied) as a main course for lunch or as a first course for dinner. The sun, the sea, the earth, and few calories!

12 whole small red snappers (about ½ pound each)
2 quarts water
1 teaspoon salt
1 large carrot, sliced
1 large onion, sliced
1 small onion stuck with 2 cloves
2 ounces Ito Wakame *(Japanese seaweed; see page 113)*
4 peppercorns
1 bunch watercress
1 cup yogurt
pepper

Wash and pat dry the fish. Set aside.

Into a sauté pan about 3½ inches deep and 12¼ inches in diameter, pour 2 quarts of water and add 1 teaspoon salt and the carrot, sliced onion, the onion stuck with the cloves, seaweed, and peppercorns. Bring to a boil and simmer for 10 minutes.

Poach the small fish 4 at a time for *4 minutes.* Carefully remove the fish to a large round platter. Arrange with their heads pointing to the center. Continue cooking the fish until all 12 are done.

With a perforated skimmer, remove the sliced onion, carrots, and seaweed. Place some onion rings on the fish. In the center where all the fish heads meet, make a mound of sliced onion and carrots, with the seaweed on top.

Strain the cooking liquid. Pour about 1 cup over the fish. Cool and refrigerate.

Wash the watercress, pat dry, and remove the stems. In a blender or food processor, purée the watercress with the yogurt. Add salt and pepper to taste and the juice of ½ a lime. Serve in a sauceboat.

Slice the rest of the lime to garnish fish platter.

Yield: 12 or 6 servings
Total calories: 1,590

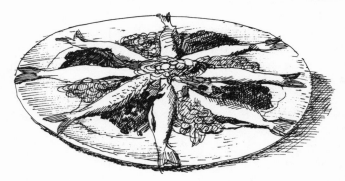

Lotte with Fennel

I never knew much about fish when I was growing up. Fish came to the table already cooked and that was that. When I came to this country, the only fish I could easily spot in a market were flounder, sole, and skate. But my son became a passionate fisherman. Summer after summer he would go fishing and we would discover the marvels of the sea. He, however, never ate fish! One day he came home with the ugliest fish I had ever seen. Its head was enormous, spiky, and flat. When I refused to deal with such an ugly fish, my son told me in a very offended way that it was a *lotte* or anglerfish, that it was great, and that even he would eat it. I cooked it, we tried it, he ate it, and it was superb. Anglerfish is plentiful in American waters but not too commonly found in fish markets. If you don't have a friend who is a fisherman or a fish store that will carry it, you can replace it in this recipe with any white fish steak.

2 pounds lotte *or anglerfish*
½ lemon
2 fennel bulbs
1 celery stalk
1 carrot
2 shallots
½ cup dry white wine
⅓ cup white wine vinegar
4 parsley sprigs
10 peppercorns
3 cups water
2 egg yolks
1 teaspoon cornstarch
⅓ cup yogurt
salt and pepper

Wash and pat dry the fish and cut it into 3-inch pieces. Slice the lemon.

Make the court-bouillon. Cut the fennel bulbs into julienne strips. Cut the celery into 1-inch pieces. Slice the carrot thin. Peel and chop the shallots. In a large saucepan place all the vegetables, and the white wine, vinegar, parsley, peppercorns, and water. Bring to a boil, lower the heat, and simmer for 5 minutes.

Arrange the slices of lemon in a steamer, place the fish on top, and steam it, covered, over the court-bouillon for 10 minutes. Remove the fish to a heated platter, with the lemon slices, and keep warm while making the sauce.

Strain the court-bouillon through a fine sieve into a bowl. Reserve the vegetables. Beat together the egg yolks and cornstarch and slowly add 2 cups of the court-bouillon. Pour into a saucepan, add the yogurt, and heat slowly, stirring all the while. Correct the seasoning and simmer until the sauce thickens.

Pour the sauce over the fish, spoon the reserved vegetables around it, and serve.

Yield: 6 servings
Total calories: 1,715

Braised Swordfish with Orange and Lime Peel

2-pound swordfish steak
2 limes
2 small hot pimentos, chopped
8 small onions
2 shallots
2 small zucchini
4 small plum tomatoes
2 tablespoons olive oil
1 orange
salt and pepper
2 tablespoons chopped fresh basil leaves for garnish
2 tablespoons chopped parsley for garnish

Wash and pat dry the fish and put it in a large bowl. Peel the zest of the limes, reserve, and squeeze the limes. Add the juice to the fish with the chopped hot pimentos. Marinate for 1 hour.

Meanwhile, peel the onions. Peel and chop the shallots. Wash the zucchini and cut them into 1-inch pieces. Peel, seed, and quarter the tomatoes.

In a casserole heat the oil and when it is hot add the onions and shallots. Cook for 4 minutes, then add the fish and brown on both sides. Reserve the marinade.

Peel the zest of the orange, reserve, and squeeze the orange. Mix the juice with the marinade and add to the fish. Add the zucchini and tomatoes and simmer, covered, for 35 minutes.

Cut the lime and orange zests into a fine julienne and add to the fish. Correct the seasoning and simmer for another 10 minutes or until the fish is done. Sprinkle with the chopped basil and parsley and serve as is from the casserole, with boiled noodles.

Yield: 4 to 6 servings
Total calories: 1,800

Fresh Salmon with Gnocchi

Italian gnocchi are potato dumplings that look like small corks scored all the way around with narrow grooves. They are available fresh or frozen in Italian pasta stores and in some supermarkets. They cook very quickly.

2 cups water + 1 quart
1 onion stuck with a clove
2 garlic cloves, sliced
salt and pepper
2 large slices fresh salmon, about 1 inch thick (1 pound)
Fresh Tomato Sauce (page 225)
1 sweet red pepper, seeded and chopped
1 green pepper, seeded and chopped
1 teaspoon chopped fresh dill
1 package gnocchi (about 1 pound)
chopped parsley for garnish

Into a large skillet pour 2 cups water and add the onion, sliced garlic, and salt and pepper. Bring to a boil, reduce the heat, and simmer for 10 minutes. Then add the salmon steaks and poach them for 7 to 8 minutes. Remove with a slotted spoon to a plate. Cool, then remove the skin and bones and cut the salmon into bite-size pieces.

Throw out the bouillon in the skillet. In the hot skillet combine the tomato sauce and chopped peppers and cook for 5 minutes, then turn off the heat. Add the pieces of salmon, correct the seasoning, and add the fresh dill. Keep warm.

In a large saucepan bring 1 quart of water to a boil with 1 teaspoon salt. Add the gnocchi, bring to a boil again, then turn off the heat and drain. Put the gnocchi in a large serving bowl, pour the tomato and salmon sauce over them, and serve garnished with parsley.

Yield: 4 servings
Total calories: 1,890

Salmon Trout with Asparagus Tips

4 salmon trout fillets (about 1 pound)
lettuce leaves
1½ pounds large asparagus
4 tablespoons yogurt
juice of ½ lime
salt and pepper
fresh dill for garnish

Wash and pat dry the fish fillets. Line a steamer with the lettuce leaves, place the fish on top, and steam, covered, for 5 minutes or until the fish is done (when it flakes easily when pricked with a fork). Keep warm.

Cut off about 4 inches of the bottom part of the asparagus and peel the asparagus. Steam it, covered, for 5 minutes.

In a small saucepan heat the yogurt with the lime juice. Add salt and pepper to taste.

Place the fish fillets on a platter, sprinkle with pepper, add the asparagus tips, pour the yogurt over them, and snip some dill on top. Serve with boiled potatoes.

Yield: 4 servings
Total calories: 1,220

Sea Trout Fillets in Lime Sauce

Ask the fishmonger to give you the trout heads and central bones. These are excellent to make a stock in which to poach the fish.

8 trout fillets (about 2 pounds) + fish heads and bones
1 onion stuck with a clove
1 carrot, sliced
1 bay leaf
parsley sprigs
salt and pepper
2 quarts water
1 soft bean curd cake

4 tablespoons yogurt
2 limes
1-inch piece fresh ginger, grated

In a large saucepan place the fish heads and bones, add the onion, carrot, bay leaf, parsley, and salt and pepper. Add 2 quarts of water, bring to a boil, then reduce the heat, and simmer for 10 minutes. Add the fish and poach for 5 minutes. Carefully remove the fish to a serving platter and keep warm while making the sauce.

In a food processor, place the bean curd, yogurt, and ½ cup of the fish stock. Run the machine until the bean curd is puréed. Slowly add the juice of 1½ limes while the machine is running.

Correct the seasoning, add the grated ginger, and pour the sauce over the fish. Garnish with lime slices.

Yield: 4 servings
Total calories: 1,740

Colette's Frozen Dinner

I never buy frozen food. I suppose it is a question of habit and taste. No frozen foods can match the flavor of fresh ingredients. But there are two things that I do use frozen, boned trout and tiny green peas. Combined they make an excellent dinner on days when unexpected guests arrive or you leave your work too late to go shopping.

4 frozen boned trout
2 packages frozen tiny green peas
4 tomatoes, peeled, quartered, and seeded
2 shallots, chopped
salt and pepper
1 tablespoon chopped fresh thyme or ½ tablespoon dried
      thyme
1 tablespoon butter
½ cup dry white wine
½ cup chicken bouillon
1 lemon for garnish

Leave the trout to thaw at room temperature for 1 hour.

Preheat the oven to 375°. Put the peas in a sieve and run under cold water to defrost. Drain well. In a baking dish place the peas, tomatoes, and shallots, mixed together. Sprinkle with salt and pepper.

Wipe the trout and sprinkle with salt and pepper inside and out. Rub them with the thyme and place on top of the vegetables. Dot with the butter and add the wine and bouillon. Bake in the 375° oven for 15 minutes, or until the trout is done. Garnish with lemon wedges and serve.

Yield: 4 servings
Total calories: 1,615

Steamed Shad Fillets with Garlic Sauce

4 shad fillets (about 1 pound)
iceberg lettuce leaves
fresh dill sprigs
8 large garlic cloves, peeled
2 egg yolks
3 tablespoons olive oil
1 cup yogurt
¼ teaspoon cayenne pepper
salt and pepper
chopped parsley or watercress for garnish
6 slices Italian bread, toasted

Wash and pat dry the shad fillets. Line a steamer with iceberg lettuce leaves. Place the fish fillets on top and add some dill sprigs. Steam, covered, for 5 to 8 minutes, depending on the thickness of the fillets. When cooked, remove the fish to a serving platter and keep warm. Discard the lettuce and dill.

In a mortar pound the garlic with a pestle until puréed. Place the egg yolks and garlic in a food processor and run the machine until the egg yolks are pale in color, then slowly add the oil. Remove to a bowl and add the yogurt, stirring with a wooden spoon. Correct the seasoning with the cayenne and salt and pepper and mix well.

Cover the fish with the sauce, sprinkle with chopped watercress or parsley, and serve with the toasted bread.

Yield: 4 servings
Total calories: 1,640

Fresh Tuna with Mussels

1½ pounds fresh tuna, boned
18 large mussels in their shells
1 cup dry white wine
1 tablespoon olive oil
2 tablespoons good wine vinegar
2 hot green peppers, chopped
2 sweet red peppers, seeded
2 sweet green peppers, seeded
8 small whole onions, peeled

4 skewers for broiling

Remove the skin from the fish and cut the fish into 2-inch cubes. Place in a large bowl. Scrape and wash the mussels, remove the beards, and soak the mussels in cold water for ½ hour, changing the water a few times.

Drain the mussels, put them in a large kettle over high heat, and shake the pot from time to time until the mussels are open (about 8 to 10 minutes). Discard any that do not open. Remove mussels from their shells and add to the tuna. Strain the cooking juice through a very fine sieve and add to the tuna. Add the wine, olive oil, vinegar, and hot peppers. Mix well, cover, and refrigerate for 2 hours.

Cut the red and green peppers into 2-inch pieces. Take a skewer and start with a piece of red pepper, add a cube of tuna, then a piece of green pepper, then a mussel, then an onion, and so on until the skewer is filled. Continue the same way with the other skewers. Broil for 6 minutes under a hot broiler or over charcoal, basting from time to time with the marinade.

Serve with steamed yellow squash.

Yield: 4 servings
Total calories: 1,550

Fish Quenelles with Morels

Morels, the French *morilles,* are those extraordinary mushrooms that look like small black sponges. Walking in an old cemetery in Massachusetts, I once found them under oak trees. Walking through a forest, you may be lucky and stumble on a whole crop. *Morilles* are imported fresh to this country and can be found in the spring and summer in specialty stores. They also can be found dried, but these should be soaked overnight. Change the water twice. When you are ready to use them, drain the *morilles* through a fine sieve, reserving the water to make the sauce.

> *7 ounces dried morels*
> *1¾ pounds fish fillets (flounder, tilefish, haddock, etc.)*
> *1 cup white bread without the crust, soaked in 2*
> *   tablespoons milk*
> *¼ pound soy butter (see Note)*
> *2 eggs, separated*
> *salt and pepper*
> *nutmeg*
> *3 quarts water*
> *2 tablespoons flour*
> *2 tablespoons butter*
> *1 cup yogurt*
> *juice of ½ lemon*

Soak the morels overnight, changing the water twice.

In a food processor, place the fish fillets, cut into 1-inch pieces, the bread with the milk, and the soy butter cut into 1-inch pieces. Run the machine until all the ingredients are puréed. Remove to a bowl.

Separate the eggs. Add the yolks to the fish mixture and mix well. Beat the egg whites until stiff. Add salt and pepper and a pinch of nutmeg to the fish mixture and mix well. Then gently fold the egg whites into the fish mixture. Refrigerate.

Heat 3 quarts of water in a large saucepan with 1 tablespoon salt. Bring to a boil, then lower the heat barely to a simmer.

Sprinkle your work table with flour. Take a large spoonful of the fish mixture, drop it on the flour and, gently, with the palm of your hand, roll it to form a 4-inch sausage or quenelle. Set aside. Continue forming quenelles until all the fish mixture has been used.

Gently drop a few quenelles at a time in the simmering water; do not crowd them. Poach for 5 minutes. The quenelles are done when they rise to the surface. The water should not boil. With a slotted spoon remove the quenelles to a serving platter and keep warm over simmering water while making the sauce.

Drain the morels, reserving the soaking water, and trim the stems; if they are very large, cut them in two. In a frying pan, melt the butter. When it is hot, add the morels and cook for 3 minutes. Then add half the water in which the morels have soaked (about ½ cup), and simmer for 5 minutes. Add salt and pepper to taste. Remove from the heat, add the yogurt, mix well, return the pan to the stove, and heat gently. Do not boil. Add the lemon, mix well again, correct the seasoning, and pour over the quenelles. Serve immediately.

Yield: 6 servings
Total calories: 2,605

NOTE: Soy butter, made with soybean oil, looks like butter and in making a batter replaces butter quite well. It is sold in health-food stores and in most Oriental vegetable stores.

Haddock Cake with Basil

If you grow basil in your garden, here is a recipe for the fall that will use the end of your crop when the leaves are quite large and the flavor very strong.

> 2 pounds ripe tomatoes
> 4 large garlic cloves
> ¼ cup chicken bouillon or fish stock
> 1½ pounds haddock, boned
> 2 cups chopped fresh basil leaves
> 6 eggs
> salt and pepper
> few drops Tabasco
> ½ tablespoon butter for the mold
> watercress for garnish
> lemon slices for garnish
> Fines Herbes Sauce (page 226)
>
> 1½-quart mold

Preheat the oven to 375°.

Dip the tomatoes in boiling water and peel, quarter, and seed them. Peel the garlic and cut into small pieces.

In a large saucepan place the tomatoes, garlic, and chicken bouillon or fish stock. Cook over medium heat, stirring from time to time, until the tomatoes are cooked and there is no liquid in the saucepan. Remove from the heat.

In a food processor place the fish, tomatoes, basil, and eggs and run the machine until all the ingredients are puréed. Correct the seasoning and add some Tabasco. Butter the mold. Pour the fish mixture into the mold and bake in the 375° oven for about 40 minutes or until a needle inserted in the center comes out clean.

Let the dish rest a few minutes, then unmold onto a platter. Garnish with watercress and sliced lemons and serve with Fines Herbes Sauce.

Yield: 8 servings
Total calories: 1,520

Giant Shrimp with Tarragon

Very large shrimp are appearing on the market. They look like miniature lobsters and their flavor is sweet and quite delicious. Serve 3 shrimp per person with steamed string beans. You should leave the heads on and not peel the shrimp; treat them as you would a lobster. These shrimp can be replaced by regular shrimp, but then they should be shelled.

> *12 giant shrimps in their shells*
> *2 tablespoons butter*
> *¼ cup brandy (optional)*
> *3 shallots, chopped*
> *3 tablespoons chopped parsley*
> *½ cup dry white wine*
> *2 cups chopped tomatoes (about 3 large tomatoes, peeled*
>   *and seeded)*
> *6 tablespoons yogurt*
> *salt and pepper*
> *1 tablespoon chopped fresh tarragon*
> *2 limes for garnish*

Wash and pat dry the shrimp. In a large frying pan—large enough to hold the shrimp side by side—heat the butter. When it is hot, add the shrimp and cook over high heat for a few minutes or until the shells turn red. Add the brandy and flame. Sprinkle the shrimp with the chopped shallots and parsley and add the wine. Mix well and add the tomatoes. Cook over medium heat for 10 minutes.

With a spatula remove the shrimp to a platter and keep warm while finishing the sauce. Add the yogurt to the sauce, correct the seasoning with salt and pepper, add the tarragon, and mix well. Heat but do not boil.

Garnish the shrimp with slices of lime and serve the sauce alongside.

Yield: 4 servings
Total calories: 1,005

Salad of Crayfish and Asparagus

Écrevisse is the French name for crayfish, the marvelous little freshwater animal that resembles a tiny lobster. They are delicious hot, cold, in salads. They are difficult to find in much of the United States, but in Louisiana, Texas, parts of the Midwest, and some other parts of the country they are plentiful. One summer we rented a house in Massachusetts that had a small pond. We decided to experiment and one of the children dropped a piece of meat in the water. As we looked down, we soon saw hundreds of small crayfish fighting for it. We bought a crayfish trap, placed a piece of pork in it, left it in the pond for a few days, and then had a feast of crayfish. If you have a pond, perhaps it has crayfish you can catch; it is worth the trouble.

If you have no supply of crayfish you can use this recipe to make a salad of large shrimp. If you can find them with their heads on, so much the better, and do not shell them.

3 dozen crayfish or large shrimp in their shells.
5 cups water
1½ pounds asparagus
1 large head chicory
Parsley Sauce (page 224)
2 tablespoons chopped chives for garnish
grated zest of 1 lemon for garnish

Wash the crayfish under cold running water. In a large kettle bring 5 cups of water to a boil, and add the crayfish. When the water boils again, boil for 2 minutes, turn off the heat, and drain the crayfish. Set aside.

Wash the asparagus and cut 3 inches from the bottoms of the stalks. Steam the asparagus, covered, for 10 minutes. Wash the chicory, trim, tear the larger leaves into pieces, and pat dry.

Line a large round serving platter with the salad. Place the crayfish on top in a circle around the edge of the platter. Place the asparagus in the center and sprinkle them with the lemon zest and chives.

Serve the salad with the sauce on the side.

Yield: 6 servings
Total calories: 305

Soft-shelled Crabs with Lime Sauce

June is crab month and soft-shelled crabs are by far the best. Allow 2 crabs per person. Serve this dish with a crisp green salad and a dry white wine, and you have a dinner fit for a king.

2 limes
4 eggs
¼ cup chopped fresh basil leaves
salt and pepper
2-inch piece fresh ginger
8 soft-shelled crabs, ready to cook
parsley for garnish

Grate the zest of the limes and set aside.

Into a bowl, squeeze the limes. Beat together the lime juice and the eggs. Cook the eggs in the top of a double boiler over simmering water, whisking all the time, until they thicken into a sauce. Remove from the heat, add the basil, grated lime zest, and salt and pepper, and keep warm over the hot water.

Grate the ginger. Place the crabs side by side in a steamer, place some grated ginger on top of each crab, and steam, covered, for 8 minutes. Serve on individual plates. Garnish with parsley and pour some sauce on the side.

Yield: 4 servings
Total calories: 875

Crab Stew

For this recipe you will need plenty of paper napkins, guests who do not mind using their fingers, and finger bowls of hot water with lime slices for your guests to wash their hands after having enjoyed this stew.

1 tablespoon salt
12 small live crabs (4 to 6 inches across)
1 tablespoon oil

3 garlic cloves, peeled and crushed
1 onion, chopped
1 jar sweet red pimentos (4 pimentos), chopped
1 fresh hot red pepper, seeded and chopped
¼ cup lime juice
1 cup chicken bouillon
2 packages tiny frozen peas, thawed
18 imported Spanish green olives stuffed with pimentos,
*   drained*
salt and pepper
2 tablespoons chopped parsley for garnish

Fill a large kettle with water and add 1 tablespoon salt. When the water boils, plunge in the live crabs and cook for 5 minutes. Drain and cool. With a cleaver, quarter the crabs.

In a large saucepan heat the oil and add the garlic, chopped onion, pimentos, hot pepper, lime juice, and bouillon. Cook for 5 minutes, then add the crabs and simmer for another 5 minutes over low heat. Now add the peas and the olives and cook until they are heated through. Correct the seasoning and sprinkle with the parsley.

Serve with fresh pasta.

Yield: 6 servings
Total calories: 1,250

Crab Salad with Cabbage and Chinese String Beans

8-ounce can crab meat
1 pound Chinese string beans (page 200)
salt and pepper
1 green spring cabbage
1 tablespoon olive oil
2 garlic cloves, chopped
1 tablespoon dark soy sauce

¼ cup red wine
1 tablespoon lime juice
2 tablespoons chopped chives for garnish

Drain the crab meat and remove any bits of shell. Set aside.

Wash and drain the string beans and cut in two. Steam the beans, covered, for 5 minutes. Sprinkle with salt and pepper and set aside.

Remove the center core of the cabbage and separate and wash the leaves. Place the cabbage leaves in a large saucepan, cover with boiling water, bring to a boil again, and turn off the heat. Drain immediately, cool under cold running water, and drain again. Remove the tough center spines of the leaves and cut the leaves into strips.

In a skillet heat the oil and add the garlic, soy sauce, wine, and cabbage. Sauté for 2 minutes, stirring with a wooden spoon, over high heat. Remove from the heat.

Line a bowl with the string beans intertwined to form a nest. Remove the cabbage with its sauce to a bowl. Add the crab meat and lime juice and correct the seasoning. Toss very gently. Place the mixture in the center of the nest of beans and sprinkle with the chopped chives.

Serve at room temperature.

Yield: 4 to 6 servings
Total calories: 565

Mussels with Leeks

2 quarts mussels in their shells
2 pounds leeks
1 tablespoon butter
salt and pepper
pinch of nutmeg
2 tablespoons cornstarch
¼ cup chicken bouillon or juice from the mussels
2 tablespoons grated Swiss cheese
2 cups milk
1 tablespoon chopped dill
juice of ½ lemon
2 tablespoons chopped parsley for garnish

Wash and scrub the mussels and remove the beards. Soak the mussels for ½ hour in cold water, changing the water a few times.

Wash the leeks carefully. Cut off most of the green part. (It can be used to make soup.) Slice the leeks. In a skillet melt the butter, add the leeks, and sauté over low heat. Sprinkle with salt and pepper and a pinch of nutmeg. Simmer for 15 minutes, stirring from time to time.

Drain the mussels, place in a large saucepan over high heat, and shake the saucepan occasionally until the mussels open (about 8 to 10 minutes). Discard any that do not open. Remove the mussels to a bowl to cool and drain the juice through a very fine sieve.

Put the cornstarch in a bowl and dilute with some of the chicken bouillon or mussel juice. Add the cornstarch mixture and the remaining bouillon or mussel juice to the leeks. Add the milk and grated cheese and cook, stirring, until the sauce thickens, about 5 minutes. Add the dill and additional pepper.

Remove the mussels from their shells and add to the sauce. Correct the seasoning and add the lemon juice. Heat. Sprinkle with chopped parsley and serve with steamed potatoes.

Yield: 4 to 6 servings
Total calories: 1,415

Squid in Tomato Sauce

One afternoon my husband, some friends, and I went to Ellis Island. My husband was then studying the possibilities of designing a conference hotel with a coffee shop, a restaurant, etc., on the island. The weather was superb (it had been boiling hot in Manhattan) and we sat on the grass looking at the city skyline and talked about food. Not just any food—we talked about squid. Squid fried, sautéed, steamed with sauce, without, Japanese style. We got so hungry that on our way back home we stopped in Chinatown, bought 6 pounds of squid, and all got in my kitchen and made squid several different ways. Serve this dish with a cool white wine, a tomato salad, and a bowl of cherries. What a feast!

3 pounds medium-size squid, cleaned (see Note)
3 garlic cloves
1 tablespoon oil
two 16-ounce cans stewed tomatoes
10 fresh basil leaves, coarsely chopped
2 tablespoons dried oregano
salt and pepper
2 tablespoons capers
1 lemon, sliced

Slice the cleaned squid, wash under running cold water, drain in a colander, then pat dry with paper towels. Steam, covered, for 4 to 5 minutes. Remove to a bowl and keep warm.

Peel and chop the garlic. In a large frying pan heat the oil and sauté the garlic. Add all the stewed tomatoes and their juice to the frying pan and mix well. Add the basil leaves, oregano, and salt and pepper, and mix well. Cook over high heat for 5 minutes, stirring all the while. Then reduce the heat and cook for 10 minutes more, stirring from time to time.

Correct the seasoning and add the squid. Heat, add the capers, mix well, and serve with the sliced lemon.

Yield: 6 servings
Total calories: 1,595

NOTE: There are squid of various sizes in the market. The medium size, about 6 to 8 inches long, I think are the best. If you shop in an Italian fish store, ask for *calamari*. Some stores sell them already cleaned and sliced. If the squid have not been cleaned: Remove the head with the bone, which is inside. Rinse the squid under cold running water before slicing.

Steamed Squid with Coriander Sauce

> 3 pounds medium-size squid, cleaned (see Note, preceding
>   recipe)
> ⅓ cup lime juice
> 4 shallots, chopped
> ¼ teaspoon grated fresh ginger
> ¾ cup watercress leaves
> 10 coriander leaves (Chinese parsley)
> ½ cup yogurt
> salt and pepper
> 2 lemons for garnish

Wash the squid and pat dry with paper towels. Cut the squid into slices ¼ inch thick. Place the squid in a steamer and steam, covered, for 4 to 5 minutes. Remove to a platter and refrigerate to cool.

Make the sauce. Place all the other ingredients except the lemons in a blender or food processor and run the machine until the ingredients are chopped fine. Correct the seasoning. Remove to a bowl.

Garnish the squid with slices of lemon and serve the sauce alongside.

Yield: 6 servings
Total calories: 1,375

Frogs' Legs with Ito Wakame

Ito Wakame is a long, dried seaweed imported from Japan, which I use in many recipes in this book. Soak in water for 5 minutes, then drain and refrigerate until ready to use.

> *1 pound frogs' legs*
> *1 tablespoon soy sauce*
> *½ teaspoon sesame oil*
> *5 drops Oriental hot oil*
> *1 ounce* Ito Wakame
> *2 garlic cloves, chopped*
> *4 scallions, sliced*
> *lettuce leaves*
> *juice of ½ lime*

Cut the pairs of frogs' legs apart, then cut each leg in two at the joint. Put all the pieces in a bowl and add the soy sauce, sesame oil, and hot oil. Marinate for 1 hour. Line a steamer with the seaweed. Remove frogs' legs from marinade, reserving the liquid. Place the frogs' legs on top of the seaweed and steam, covered, for 5 minutes. Remove from the steamer to a platter.

Cut the seaweed in several pieces, place in a bowl, and add the chopped garlic and the marinade. Toss well and add the scallions.

Place 1 or 2 perfect lettuce leaves on each serving plate. Fill with the seaweed, place the frogs' legs on top, sprinkle with lime juice, and serve.

Yield: 4 servings
Total calories: 315

Snail Pie with Spinach

When I discovered that snails have few calories, I jumped with joy. I love snails, but suddenly I realized, snails with no butter, what a disaster! Then one day I came up with this recipe. It does not have the wonderful smell of cooking butter, garlic, and parsley, but it is very good.

> *2 pounds fresh spinach*
> *1 large can snails (24 snails)*
> *4 shallots, chopped*
> *½ cup dry white wine*
> *1 tablespoon dried tarragon*
> *4 egg yolks*
> *½ cup yogurt*
> *salt and pepper*
> Pâte Brisée *(page 233)*
> *¼ teaspoon butter for quiche pan*
> *2 tablespoons milk*
>
> *9-inch quiche or pie pan*

Wash and drain the spinach and remove the stems. Steam the spinach, covered, for 2 minutes. Cool.

Drain the snails. In a saucepan place the snails, chopped shallots, wine, and tarragon. Bring to a boil, then reduce the heat, cover, and simmer for 30 minutes.

Beat together 3 of the egg yolks and the yogurt. Away from the heat, add the egg yolks to the snails, stirring with a metal whisk. Correct the seasoning and set aside.

Preheat the oven to 425°.

Roll out half of the pastry dough on a floured board. Butter a 9-inch quiche pan and line it with the dough. Squeeze all the water from the spinach and spread the spinach in the bottom of the pie. Add the snails with their sauce.

Roll out the remaining dough on the floured board and cover the pie. Roll and pinch the edges tightly. Beat the remaining yolk together with the milk and, with a pastry brush, brush the yolk over the pie. Bake in the 425° oven for 30 minutes, or until the piecrust is golden brown.

Serve with a tomato salad.

Yield: 6 servings
Total calories: 2,285

Salade de Coques with Spinach Mousse

Sometimes when I walk through Chinatown, I find tiny clams that the French call *coques*. They are delicious served tepid with a mousse of spinach as an appetizer—or as a main dish on a hot summer evening. You can replace the *coques* with littleneck clams or mussels, or even small bay scallops.

2 pounds small clams in their shells
2 pounds fresh spinach
2 shallots, chopped
1/2 cup yogurt
2 tablespoons strawberry or wine vinegar
1/4 teaspoon nutmeg
salt and pepper
paprika
2 tablespoons chives
2 lemons for garnish

Wash the *coques* and soak in cold water for 1 hour. Drain. Wash the spinach and remove the stems.

In a large saucepan, place the *coques* and the chopped shallots and steam, covered, until the shells open (about 6 to 8 minutes). Discard any that do not open. Remove the clams from their shells and keep warm.

Take half the spinach and blanch it in boiling water for 3 minutes. Drain, refresh under cold running water, and squeeze with your hands until all the water is removed. Place the spinach in a food processor with the yogurt, vinegar, nutmeg, and salt and pepper. Purée. Remove to a bowl and correct the seasoning.

Coarsely chop the uncooked spinach and toss with salt and pepper. On individual plates, place the *coques* in the center and surround with spinach mousse and then with the uncooked spinach. Sprinkle with paprika and the chopped chives and garnish with lemon quarters.

Yield: 4 servings
Total calories: 495

CHICKEN & TURKEY

Stuffed Cold Chicken Breast in Vine Leaves

Whenever I make a vegetable terrine I always have too many vegetables. For this recipe you can use leftover vegetables if they are
not overcooked. The chicken breasts have to be flattened so that
they can be easily rolled: To flatten a chicken breast, place it between 2 pieces of foil and pound it with the back of a heavy skillet. When the chicken rolls are cooked and cool, they are cut into
1-inch slices and served with a yogurt sauce.

> *4 boned chicken breasts*
> *1 jar vine leaves (16 leaves)*
> *salt and pepper*
> *2 garlic cloves, sliced*
> *1 large carrot, cooked and cut into julienne strips*
> *1 kohlrabi or celery root, cooked and cut into julienne*
> *   strips*
> *¼ pound string beans, cooked*
> *¼ teaspoon cumin*
> *juice of 2 limes*
> *1 cup Yogurt Sauce (page 221)*

Flatten the chicken breasts. Cut each breast in two lengthwise.
Wash the vine leaves under cold water and drain.
    Sprinkle each piece of chicken breast with salt and pepper
and rub with garlic. Place some of the carrots, kohlrabi or celery
root, and string beans in the center of each piece, sprinkle with

salt, pepper, and cumin, and add 1 slice of garlic. Roll the chicken meat tightly. Place 2 vine leaves on a flat surface, partly overlapping, and roll the chicken in the vine leaves.

Steam the chicken rolls, covered, for 6 minutes. Remove to a bowl and add the lime juice. Refrigerate until cold.

To serve, cut the stuffed rolls into 1-inch slices. Arrange the slices on a platter or a wicker basket lined with vine leaves. Serve the Yogurt Sauce alongside.

Yield: 6 servings
Total calories: 730

Stuffed Chicken Legs

This is a very elegant dish for a dinner party but it requires a butcher who will have the time and patience to bone the chicken legs for you or a very sharp knife to bone them yourself. To do that, cut the meat around the tip of the leg, then push the meat up the bone as you cut the tendons away. You are left with a pocket that you stuff with vegetables and bake with soy sauce. Allow 2 chicken legs per person.

2 carrots
½ pound string beans
salt and pepper
1 tablespoon grated fresh ginger
2 teaspoons sake
8 chicken legs, boned
2 tablespoons dark soy sauce
2 cups chicken bouillon
parsley for garnish

Preheat the oven to 375°.

Scrape and wash the carrots. Cut in two lengthwise, then cut each piece in two crosswise. Cut each piece into narrow strips. Trim the ends of the string beans and wash. Steam the carrots and beans, covered, for 4 to 5 minutes or until they are barely tender.

Remove to a bowl, sprinkle with salt and pepper, and add the grated ginger and the *sake*. Mix well and let cool.

When the vegetables are cool, fill the chicken legs with them. Arrange the chicken legs side by side in a baking pan. Rub them with the soy sauce and sprinkle with pepper. Pour ½ the chicken bouillon into the pan and bake in the 375° oven for 25 minutes, basting from time to time with the remaining bouillon. The chicken legs are done when they are golden brown and the juice runs clear when they are pricked with a fork. Remove to a serving platter, garnish with parsley, and serve.

Yield: 4 servings
Total calories: 1,090

Chicken with Spring Onions

Spring onions look like overgrown scallions and they are sweet and tender.

4 small turnips
4 spring onions
4 leeks
3-pound chicken, quartered
2 cups yogurt
¼ cup dry white vermouth
8 small baby carrots
parsley sprig
pinch of dried thyme
1 celery stalk
1 bay leaf
salt and pepper

Scrape and wash the carrots. Peel and wash the turnips. Set aside. Peel the onions, leaving about 4 inches of the green stems on. Wash the leeks carefully and leave about 2 inches of the green part. Cut in two lengthwise.

In a large saucepan place the 2 chicken thighs and add the yogurt and vermouth, the carrots and turnips, a parsley sprig, a pinch of thyme, the celery stalk cut in 1-inch pieces, and the bay leaf. Bring to a boil. Reduce the heat and simmer, skimming the surface from time to time, for 30 minutes. Then add the 2 breasts, the spring onions, and the leeks. Simmer for 20 minutes more.

Remove the chicken pieces to a serving platter and surround with the vegetables. Strain the sauce, correct the seasoning, pour over the chicken, and serve.

Yield: 4 servings
Total calories: 1,865

Sautéed Chicken with Tarragon Vinegar

3-pound chicken, cut into serving pieces
4 shallots, chopped
1 bay leaf
1 cup chicken stock
salt and pepper
1 tablespoon dried tarragon
1 cup tarragon wine vinegar
1 teaspoon sugar
¼ pound mushrooms, sliced

Put the chicken in a casserole with the chopped shallots and bay leaf and pour ½ cup of the stock over the chicken. Bring to a boil, reduce the heat, and cook until all the chicken stock has evaporated. Now brown the pieces of chicken on all sides and then add the remaining chicken stock. Sprinkle with salt, pepper, and tarragon and cook, covered, over medium heat until the chicken is done.

Remove the chicken to a platter and keep warm while making the sauce. Remove the bay leaf and add the vinegar and sugar to the juices in the casserole. Cook, uncovered, and reduce by half. Then add the mushrooms and cook for 5 minutes more. Pour the sauce over the chicken and serve.

Yield: 4 servings
Total calories: 1,295

Baked Chicken with Red Peppers

4 small onions
1 celery root
3 garlic cloves
1¾ pounds sweet red peppers
3-pound chicken, cut into serving pieces
2 tablespoons flour
2 tablespoons butter
salt and pepper
1 bunch parsley, chopped
1 cup chicken bouillon

Preheat the broiler and the oven to 425°.

Peel the onions. Peel the celery root and slice; cut each slice into 4 pieces. Peel the garlic and slice.

Cut the red peppers in two, core, remove the seeds, and place on a grill under the hot broiler. Broil until the skins are black. Dip the peppers in cold water and remove all the skins. Cut each half into strips about 1 inch wide.

Roll the chicken in the flour. In an ovenproof pan, on top of the stove, heat the butter, add the pieces of chicken, and brown on all sides. Sprinkle with salt and pepper, then add all the vegetables and the garlic and parsley. (Reserve some parsley for garnish.) Mix well. Add the chicken bouillon.

Bake in the 425° oven for 40 minutes, basting from time to time. Add water if the bouillon is not sufficient.

Serve sprinkled with chopped parsley.

Yield: 4 servings
Total calories: 1,795

Broiled Dodoma Chicken

Dodoma, the new capital of Tanzania, is located in the center of the country on a high plateau. During the rainy season, roads are impassable and food has a hard time reaching the town. The people have to rely on what is grown and raised around Dodoma. I spent a few months in Dodoma during that period. Chickens were available and tomatoes, onions, and the Indian spices, which could be found in all the Indian groceries scattered around the marketplace. Tired of having plain broiled chicken for a week, I asked one of my Indian neighbors how she cooked her chickens. She gave me several recipes and this one was the best. The chickens should be quite small, split in two, one half per person.

2 small broilers, split (about 2 pounds each)
juice of 2 limes
2 hot green peppers, chopped fine
2-inch piece of fresh ginger, grated
2 tablespoons coriander seeds
1 teaspoon coarse salt
½ teaspoon ground cloves
2 tablespoons butter at room temperature
watercress for garnish

Put the broilers on a platter, pour the lime juice over them, and sprinkle with the chopped hot peppers. Marinate for 1 hour.

In a mortar pound together the ginger, coriander seeds, salt, and ground cloves until all the spices are pulverized. (You can do the same in a blender.) Mix the spices with the butter.

Carefully loosen the skin from the four chicken breasts and insert some of the spiced butter. Cut a ½-inch slit on the thighs and insert some of the butter. Rub the chicken all over with the remaining butter. Preheat a broiler or a charcoal grill. Broil the chickens on the inside first, about 3 inches from the heat, for 10 minutes, then turn them over and broil the skin side for another 10 to 12 minutes, or until the juice runs clear when the thighs are pricked with a fork.

Serve the chickens on a platter garnished with watercress.

Yield: 4 servings
Total calories: 1,380

Roast Chicken

4- to 5-pound roasting chicken
4 large Chinese dried mushrooms
1 cup cold water
2 tablespoons dark soy sauce
salt and pepper
1 cup chicken bouillon
3 bunches watercress

Preheat oven 425°.

Pat the chicken dry and remove any loose fat. Place the chicken in a roasting pan. Soak the Chinese mushrooms in 1 cup of cold water for 20 minutes. Drain the mushrooms but reserve the water. Cut off their stems and discard.

Detach the chicken skin from its breast by sliding your fingers between the two. Slide 2 mushrooms under the skin of the breast on each side of the chicken. Rub the chicken with soy sauce and sprinkle inside with salt and pepper.

Pour the chicken bouillon around the chicken and bake in the 425° oven for 1½ hours, basting from time to time.

Wash the watercress and cut off the stems. When the chicken has been in the oven for 1 hour, place the watercress around the chicken and add the water from the mushrooms. There should be about 1 cup of liquid in the pan. Add more water if necessary.

The chicken is done when the juice runs clear when the thigh is pricked with a fork. Remove the chicken to a carving board, carve it, and arrange on a serving platter. Pour all the juice from the pan, with the watercress, into a large bowl. Let it stand for 5 minutes, then skim off the fat with a spoon. Pour the juice and the watercress over the carved chicken and serve.

If you wish, you can put the skimmed juice with the watercress in a blender and blend until reduced to a cream, then pour over the chicken.

Yield: 6 servings
Total calories: 2,660

Roast Chicken with Clementines

Clementines are small tangerines whose name originated on the Riviera or in North Africa. The most famous ones are from Algeria and Nice. They are now appearing in greater quantities in the United States. Their skin is thin, peels easily, and the segments are seedless. The flavor of the fruit is delicate, yet a little bit spicy and tart.

4- to 5-pound roasting chicken
salt and pepper
12 clementines
2 tablespoons mushroom soy sauce
1½ cups water
parsley for garnish

Preheat the oven to 375°.

Prepare the chicken: Remove all loose fat, and sprinkle inside with pepper and lightly with salt. Peel the clementines and chop the skins in a food processor or blender. Loosen the skin of the chicken around the breast. Place 2 tablespoons of the chopped clementine skins under the chicken skin. Rub the chicken with the soy sauce and stuff it with 4 clementines.

Put the chicken in a roasting pan and surround it with the remaining clementines. Add the water to the pan and roast for 1½ hours or until the juice runs clear when the chicken's thigh is pricked with a fork. Baste frequently.

Carve the chicken, arrange on a platter, and surround with the clementines and the parsley. Keep warm.

Pour the sauce into a small saucepan. Let it stand while you carve the chicken. Remove the fat, which will float to the top, with a spoon. Add ½ cup water, reheat, and serve with the chicken.

Yield: 6 to 8 servings
Total calories: 3,445

Chicken with Potatoes and Tomatoes "Dauphinoise"

4 boned chicken breasts
salt and pepper
6 large potatoes
pinch of nutmeg
6 garlic cloves, sliced
4 ripe tomatoes, sliced
3 large onions, sliced
5 thin slices Swiss cheese
2 cups chicken bouillon

Preheat the oven to 325°.

Cut the chicken breasts into strips about ½ inch wide. Sprinkle with salt and pepper and set aside. Peel the potatoes, cut into slices about ⅛ inch thick, and soak in cold water to prevent them from getting brown. Drain and pat dry.

Line the bottom of an ovenproof baking dish with half the sliced potatoes and sprinkle with salt and pepper and nutmeg. Cover with the chicken strips, then with the slices of garlic and tomato. Sprinkle again with salt and pepper, then cover with the sliced onion. Add the remaining potatoes and cover with the slices of cheese.

Pour the chicken bouillon over all, cover with foil, and bake in the 325° oven for 1 hour. Then remove the foil, raise the heat to 375°, and cook for ½ hour more or until the cheese is golden brown and the top layer of potatoes is crisp.

Serve garnished with chopped parsley.

Yield: 6 servings
Total calories: 2,050

Chicken with Pomegranate

This recipe was brought back to me by my nephew John after he had spent two months in Iraq. When he made it for us, it was much too sweet, although he said that this was the way his Iraqi friends did it. I adapted the recipe, using less sugar and more pomegranate. Pomegranate is a tropical fruit, but it is found in the United States and looks like a large red apple. It has thousands of small seeds inside, filled with juice. Rub your hands with lemon first before removing the seeds, as they will stain your fingers.

2 onions, chopped
2 cups chicken bouillon
4 boned chicken breasts
2 pomegranates
¼ cup orange juice
1 tablespoon lemon juice
¼ cup sugar
pinch of nutmeg
½ cup chopped walnuts
salt and pepper

In a saucepan place the chopped onions and chicken bouillon. Bring to a boil, reduce the heat, and add the chicken breasts. Simmer for 10 minutes. Remove the chicken and keep warm while making the sauce.

Seed both pomegranates. Put ½ the seeds in a fine sieve and press with a wooden spoon over a bowl to get the juice. (You can also buy pomegranate juice or press the fruit in a juicer if you have one.) You should have 1½ cups juice.

In a saucepan place the pomegranate juice, orange and lemon juice, sugar, nugmeg, and walnuts. Cook over low heat for 15 minutes. Add salt and pepper, then the remaining pomegranate seeds. Heat through. Cut the chicken breasts lengthwise into 1-inch strips and arrange on a platter. Pour the sauce over them and serve with steamed rice.

Yield: 6 servings
Total calories: 1,580

Steamed Chicken with Vegetable Sauce

In some Chinese grocery stores you can find a rice-paper wrapper about 10 inches in diameter. It comes from Thailand and is perfect for wrapping food that is to be steamed. It is very low in calories. Once cooked, it seems to disappear, but the food is still held together by a transparent film. This rice paper is called *Banh Trang Mong Va Deo,* or simply ask for rice paper. Soak it in water to soften it, then wrap it around anything you wish to steam. It can be replaced by lettuce or cabbage leaves, blanched before using.

> *4 boned chicken breasts*
> *salt and pepper*
> *6 round sheets rice paper*
> *12 fresh basil leaves*
> *2-inch piece fresh ginger, grated*
> *1 lemon, sliced, for garnish*
> *1½ cups Vegetable Sauce (page 222)*

Slice each chicken breast lengthwise into 3 pieces. Sprinkle with salt and pepper. Soak the rice paper in water. Place 1 sheet on a flat surface, put 2 slices of chicken on top, and add 2 basil leaves and some of the fresh grated ginger. Fold the rice paper to envelop the chicken and proceed the same way until all the chicken breast has been used.

Steam, covered, for 5 minutes. Remove carefully to a serving platter, surround with slices of lemon, and serve with the Vegetable Sauce, hot, on the side.

Yield: 6 servings
Total calories: 700

Chicken Breast Baked with Capers and Mustard

4 boned chicken breasts
1 tablespoon soy sauce
1 tablespoon Dijon mustard
2 tablespoons imported capers
salt and pepper
½ cup chicken bouillon
parsley for garnish

Preheat the oven to 450°.
    Wipe the chicken breast and remove the skin. In an oven-proof dish, place the chicken breasts side by side, rub them with soy sauce, then spread mustard on top. Add the capers, salt lightly, and sprinkle with pepper. Pour the chicken bouillon over all. Bake in the 450° oven for 15 minutes. Garnish with parsley and serve with a steamed vegetable.

Yield: 4 servings
Total calories: 380

Soybeans with Chicken Balls

1 pound soybeans
2 cups chicken bouillon
2 tablespoons soy sauce
3 garlic cloves
salt and pepper
4 boned chicken breasts, cubed
1½ tablespoons sesame oil
2 eggs
*1 Chinese cabbage (*bok choy; see page 159*)*
1 onion, chopped
¼ cup water
½ cup fresh bean sprouts

Soak the soybeans in water overnight. Drain off whatever water is left the next day.

In a saucepan place the soybeans and add the chicken bouillon plus enough water to cover the beans, the soy sauce, and 1 garlic clove, crushed. Add salt and pepper, bring to a boil, then lower the heat and simmer until the soybeans are tender, about 45 minutes.

Put the cubed chicken breasts in a food processor and run the machine until the chicken is chopped fine. Remove to a bowl and add the remaining garlic, ½ tablespoon of the sesame oil, the eggs, and salt and pepper, and mix well. Form balls with the chicken mixture about the size of a large walnut.

Wash the cabbage and cut it into bite-size pieces.

In a skillet heat the remaining tablespoon of sesame oil, add the chopped onion, and sauté for 4 minutes. Then add the chicken balls and brown them on all sides. Add the cabbage, sauté for another 4 minutes, then add ¼ cup water and cook for 5 more minutes. Correct the seasoning and turn off the heat.

Put the soybeans on a large serving platter, place the chicken on top with the cabbage, and sprinkle with bean sprouts.

Yield: 6 servings
Total calories: 2,730

Couscous with Braised Chicken in Coriander Sauce

Couscous is a North African dish made with cracked wheat, which is steamed and served with either a lamb or chicken stew. I have adapted this recipe. Here the chicken is braised with a coriander sauce.

1 tablespoon coarse salt
4-pound chicken, cut into serving pieces
⅓ cup lime juice
2 shallots, chopped

¼ teaspoon grated fresh ginger
¾ cup watercress leaves
10 coriander leaves (Chinese parsley)
2 cups yogurt
pepper
Steamed Couscous (recipe follows)

Heat a heavy-bottomed skillet to which you have added 1 table-spoon coarse salt. Add the chicken pieces and sauté in their own fat for a few minutes until the chicken is brown on all sides.

Purée all the remaining ingredients, except the couscous, in a food processor. Add this yogurt sauce to the chicken in the skillet, and lower the heat. Simmer for 30 minutes, stirring from time to time. Serve with the Steamed Couscous.

Yield: 6 servings
Total calories: 1,850

Steamed Couscous

4 cups dry couscous (1 package)
4 cups boiling water
2 tablespoons butter
salt and pepper

Stir together the couscous and the boiling water until all the water is absorbed.

Line a steamer with a Handy Wipe towel (the couscous grain is very small), or use a *couscousière* (a special pot made for cooking couscous). Place the couscous on the Handy Wipe and steam, covered, for 5 minutes. Remove to a bowl, add the butter, salt, and pepper, and fluff with a fork. Serve with chicken or lamb.

Yield: 6 servings
Total calories: 2,420

Fricassee of Turkey on a Bed of Leeks

Stories abound in French cuisine about where and when turkeys appeared in Europe. The best ones are to be found in Alexandre Dumas' *Le Grand Dictionnaire de la Cuisine*. Among other stories he tells, he says that turkeys should feel offended at being called "the creatures of the Jesuits," even if history does tell us that it was the Jesuits who brought the turkey to Europe from the Americas. Personally, I didn't use to like turkeys. I always thought, like Brillat-Savarin, that turkeys were foreigners and that nothing looked more like my aging uncle Theodore's neck than a live turkey. But a good, white, fresh turkey, not too big, well prepared, is delicious and low in calories. For this recipe, choose a small turkey. Have the butcher cut it into serving pieces, and enjoy a meal that will add nothing to your weight.

> *2 pounds leeks*
> *2 tablespoons butter*
> *pepper*
> *1 tablespoon mushroom soy sauce*
> *1 tablespoon dried rosemary*
> *9-pound turkey, cut into serving pieces*
> *½ cup bouillon*
> *chopped parsley for garnish*

Wash and trim the leeks, leaving about 2 inches of the green tops, and slice them thin. In a large covered sauté pan, 12 inches in diameter and 3½ inches deep (about 6½-quart capacity), melt the butter. When it is hot, add the sliced leeks, sauté them for a few minutes, and add pepper, soy sauce, and rosemary. Mix well. Lower the heat and simmer for 5 minutes.

Then add the turkey pieces, raise the heat, and sauté for 5 minutes, stirring all the while. Add the bouillon, lower the heat, cover, and cook for 25 minutes, or until the turkey is done. (You may have to add some water.)

Transfer the turkey pieces to a serving platter, cover with the leeks and pan juices, sprinkle with parsley, and serve.

Yield: 10 servings
Total calories: 4,810

Sliced Turkey Breast with Artichoke

Turkey breast is appearing today in most supermarkets. Well prepared, it can taste like veal scallopine at half the price and
calories. Here the turkey slices are quickly cooked in 1 tablespoon of oil or butter, then moistened with the artichoke hearts.

> *8 thin slices turkey breast (about 1½ pounds)*
> *1 tablespoon olive oil or butter*
> *10-ounce can artichoke hearts*
> *salt and pepper*
> *1 tablespoon dried tarragon*
> *parsley for garnish*

Place each turkey slice between 2 sheets of wax paper and pound
with the back of a skillet or anything heavy you have handy. The
slices should be pounded very thin.

In a large skillet heat the oil. Add the turkey slices and sauté
for a few minutes on both sides. Drain the artichokes and cut
them in two. Add them to the turkey, sprinkle with salt and pepper, and add the tarragon. Mix well, cover, and lower the heat.
Cook for 5 to 6 minutes more. Garnish with parsley and serve
with Stewed Tomatoes (page 224).

Yield: 4 servings
Total calories: 1,360

Rolled Turkey Breast with Fiddleheads
on a Bed of Taro

The title of this recipe suggests some kind of spy story set among
gypsies. In fact, it is and it isn't. Fiddleheads are a new discovery;
taro is a Chinese root, which is also eaten in South America. All
these clues put together equal a good American recipe.

Taro is a round root about 4 inches in diameter with a dark
brown skin. When cut, the inside meat is white with threads of

purple, like Italian marble (another clue). Once peeled and cut into julienne strips, it has to be washed many times as the starch it gives out is very bitter. When cooked taro tastes like potatoes (another clue), but with fewer calories.

> 1 pound fiddleheads
> 1½ pounds boned turkey breast, cut into 8 very thin slices
> salt and pepper
> 2 tablespoons fresh tarragon leaves
> 2 tablespoons butter
> 1 taro root
> 1½ cups chicken bouillon
> watercress for garnish

Preheat the oven to 450°.

Clean and wash the fiddleheads as on page 63. Spread out a slice of turkey and place 2 or 3 fiddleheads on top. Sprinkle with salt and pepper and add some tarragon leaves. Add a small piece of butter and roll tightly. Set aside and make 7 more rolls in the same way.

Peel the taro root. Cut in several pieces so they will fit the feed tube of a food processor. Shred the taro with the julienne slicing disk. Place the taro in a colander and rinse under cold running water until the water that drains out is clear.

Line a baking pan with the taro, sprinkle with salt and pepper, and place the rolled turkey breasts on top, side by side. Add the bouillon and bake for 25 minutes in the 450° oven.

Remove the turkey rolls and arrange them on a platter with the taro in the center. The taro will have the consistency of a potato purée. Garnish with watercress and serve the pan juices as a sauce alongside in a sauceboat.

Yield: 4 servings
Total calories: 1,580

Turkey Breast Cooked in Yogurt and Spices

My Egyptian grandmother used to make this recipe with lamb when she felt the lamb in the winter had a strong taste. I tried it with turkey and found that it worked even better.

1½ pounds boned turkey breast
1 pint yogurt
1 large onion
2 large garlic cloves
1-inch piece fresh ginger
2 tablespoons olive oil
4 cloves
1 tablespoon ground coriander
¼ teaspoon cayenne pepper
2 tablespoons ground almonds
salt and pepper
2 tablespoons chopped parsley

Cut the turkey breast into 1-inch cubes. Place in a bowl, cover with ½ cup of the yogurt, cover with foil, and refrigerate overnight.

Peel and chop the onion. Peel and chop the garlic. Grate the ginger.

In a large skillet heat the oil and add the onion, garlic, ginger, cloves, coriander, and cayenne pepper. Cook over low heat for 5 minutes, stirring. Then add the turkey and the remaining yogurt. Stir, add the ground almonds, stir again, and correct the seasoning. Simmer over medium heat, stirring from time to time, for 15 minutes.

Remove the meat and the sauce to a serving bowl. Sprinkle with chopped parsley. Serve over cellophane noodles or steamed rice.

Yield: 4 servings
Total calories: 1,855

Turkey Breast with Chinese Fuzzy Gourd (*Chieh Que*)

Chinese fuzzy gourd is a member of the squash family. It is covered with a fine fuzz. Rub off the fuzz with paper towels and peel off the skin before using the gourd.

> *3 Chinese fuzzy gourds*
> *1 teaspoon sesame oil*
> *1 tablespoon butter*
> *2¼ pounds boned turkey breast, cubed*
> *16-ounce can peeled tomatoes*
> *2-inch piece fresh ginger, grated*
> *1 tablespoon soy sauce*
> *10 drops Oriental hot oil*
> *parsley for garnish*

Rub the gourds, peel, and cut into 1-inch slices. Heat the sesame oil and butter in a skillet, add the turkey, and brown on all sides. Drain the tomatoes over a bowl so as to reserve the liquid. Add to the skillet the tomatoes, ginger, sliced gourd, soy sauce, and hot oil. Mix well and reduce the heat. Cook for 20 minutes, adding some of the tomato juice if necessary. Correct the seasoning and transfer to a serving platter. Garnish with parsley and serve with rice.

Yield: 6 servings
Total calories: 2,180

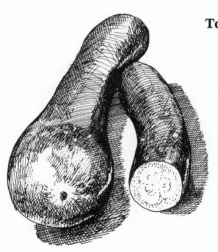

Broiled Turkey Breast with Red Plums

1 pound boned turkey breast
salt and pepper
1 tablespoon oil
8 red plums
2 tablespoons brandy
6 bay leaves
1 head romaine lettuce
½ cup Fines Herbes Sauce (page 226)

6 skewers for broiling

Cut the turkey into large cubes, place in a bowl, sprinkle with salt and pepper, and add the oil. Mix well and set aside.

Slice each plum in two and remove the pit. Place the plums in another bowl and pour the brandy over them. Cover and marinate 1 hour.

Prepare the skewers: First a piece of plum, then turkey and then plum, then a piece of bay leaf, then turkey. Repeat until all the skewers are filled, ending each with a piece of plum. Sprinkle with salt and pepper.

Broil the turkey skewers for 10 minutes under a hot broiler, turning them often. Meanwhile, wash and pat dry the romaine and cut the leaves in two. Line a long serving platter with the romaine. Place the turkey skewers on top and pour the Fines Herbes Sauce over them. Serve right away.

Yield: 4 servings
Total calories: 1,080

Charcoal-Broiled Turkey Breast with Pineapple

Last winter we went to Puerto Rico for a long weekend. We drove to the southern part of the island, which has the most spectacular clean and empty beaches and where the water is transparent. One evening as we were taking a walk along the water, we met a young Puerto Rican couple barbecuing on the beach. We started to talk to them and ended up sharing their dinner. Philippe and Maria had made this wonderful pineapple and chicken brochette. Back in New York I tried it with turkey and found it as delicious, especially when you think that a pound of pineapple is only 236 calories.

1 fresh pineapple
1½ pounds boned turkey breast
2 limes
½ tablespoon oil
salt and pepper
1 tablespoon cumin seeds, crushed

4 skewers for charcoal broiling

Peel the pineapple and cut it into 2-inch slices. Remove the center core and cut each slice into large cubes. Set aside. Cut the turkey breast into large cubes and put in a bowl. Squeeze the limes and pour the juice over the turkey. Marinate for about 2 hours.

Prepare the turkey skewers: a piece of turkey, a piece of pineapple, then turkey, and alternate until the 4 skewers are filled. Dip a brush in the oil and brush the skewers. Sprinkle with salt and pepper and roll in the crushed cumin.

Broil over charcoal 6 to 7 minutes on each side. Serve with Egyptian Rice (page 176).

Yield: 4 servings
Total calories: 1,610

QUAIL, SQUAB, DUCK & RABBIT

Quail with Potatoes Dauphinoise

In late fall I was walking through Chinatown one day when I spotted a street vendor with a big sign saying, "Quail: $1.00 a-piece." Quail in the United States are usually quite expensive so, intrigued, I stopped to look. They came from Canada; from Montreal to be exact. I bought 12 of them, called my closest friends, and served them this really spectacular dish. Later I discovered that quail today are more readily available in the winter, frozen from Canada, fresh from the United States. Serve 1 quail per person. Be sure not to overcook them, and tell your guests to use their fingers as these birds are very small and not that easy to eat—but so good!

2 pounds potatoes
1 pound large onions
salt and pepper
½ pound French Gruyère, sliced
1 cup milk
½ cup chicken bouillon
6 quail
6 large mushroom caps
parsley for garnish

Preheat the oven to 375°.

Peel and slice the potatoes. Peel and slice the onions.

Cover the bottom of a 9-inch quiche pan with sliced potatoes and cover the potatoes with sliced onions. Sprinkle with salt and pepper, and cover with 4 slices of cheese. Over the cheese put more potatoes and repeat the above sequence until all the potatoes have been used. Pour the milk and bouillon over the potatoes. Bake for 1 hour in the 375° oven.

Meanwhile, wipe the quail and rub them with salt and pepper. Wash the mushroom caps and place 1 in the cavity of each quail. When the potatoes have cooked 1 hour, place the quail on them, breasts toward the rim of the quiche pan, so the legs meet in the center. Bake for 35 minutes.

Place some parsley in the center where the quail legs meet and serve with steamed Swiss chard or a green salad.

Yield: 6 servings
Total calories: 3,315

Marinated Quail on a Bed of Steamed Glasswort

You may wonder, as I did, what on earth is glasswort. Well, glasswort is a weed that grows in salty sea marshes. I discovered it one summer when my daughter Cecile went to spend the summer at St. George's School and did some research in the marshes. Halfway through the summer we went to see her. When we walked with her through the marshes, she handed me a green branch, soft but crunchy to the touch, salty to the taste, and said, "Look, Maman, these are *Salicornia*, they are delicious steamed or raw, take some to New York." She picked a whole bag for us. I brought them home and we ate them once steamed and once in a salad, thinking all the while that our daughter had strange but wonderful taste. A year later I came upon Pamela Michael's book *All Good Things Around Us* and found out that glasswort is the common name for *Salicornia* and that it is in fact a great American delicacy. It grows on the eastern seaboard, and if you happen to spend the summer near a marsh, do try it. It is quite exceptional. The quail can be replaced by squab in the spring and summer (see Note) and the glasswort by any steamed green vegetable, perhaps very young asparagus.

8 quail
juice of 1 lime
1 teaspoon cumin
salt and pepper
1 garlic clove, crushed
½ pound glasswort
1 tablespoon butter
chopped parsley for garnish

Split the quail along the back, open them up, and place in a bowl. In a small bowl mix together the lime juice, cumin, salt and pepper, and the crushed garlic. Mix well. Pour the marinade over the quail, turn them over several times so all the birds are coated, and refrigerate for a couple of hours.

Preheat the broiler.

Wash and drain the glasswort and steam, covered, for 4 minutes. Broil the quail for 4 minutes on each side, basting with the pan juices when you turn them over.

Line a large serving platter with the glasswort. Sprinkle with pepper and the butter cut in small dice. Place the quail on top, sprinkle with chopped parsley, and serve.

Yield: 4 servings
Total calories: 2,200

NOTE: If you use squab, allow 1 per person.

Stuffed Squab with Pistachio Nuts and Vine Leaves

I love two things: squab and vine leaves. In my garden I planted a grape arbor with the idea that in the fall we would all gather in the garden, pick the grapes, set them in large vats and, after having taken a foot bath, we would all squash the grapes and make wonderful wine. Well, things didn't turn out quite this way. I have a grape arbor, millions of grape leaves, and about a bowl of grapes each fall—just enough for dessert for one dinner. Having so many leaves, I combined my dreams with squab and came up with this recipe. (Vine leaves are sold in most supermarkets in jars.)

> ½ cup rice
> 1 cup hot water
> ½ teaspoon salt
> 4 squab
> 1 lemon
> ¼ pound white mushrooms
> ¼ pound shelled pistachios
> pepper
> 1 tablespoon dried rosemary
> 8 vine leaves (½ jar)
> 2 tablespoons butter
> 1 cup chicken bouillon
> watercress for garnish

Cook the rice in a small saucepan with 1 cup of hot water and ½ teaspoon salt. Wipe the squab and rub with the lemon. Wash the mushrooms and quarter them.

When the rice is cooked, remove to a bowl. Add the mushrooms, pistachio nuts, and salt and pepper. Add the rosemary and mix well. Stuff the squab with this mixture.

Soak the vine leaves in cold water for a few minutes. Pat the leaves dry and wrap each squab in 2 leaves. Tie with a string.

In a large saucepan—large enough to hold the squab side by side—melt the butter, add the squab, and brown on all sides. Then add the chicken bouillon and salt and pepper. Reduce the heat and simmer for 25 minutes or until the squab are done (when flesh is easily pricked with a fork). Place the squab on a serving platter, remove the strings, pour the pan juices over them, and garnish with watercress.

Serve with steamed yellow squash.

Yield: 4 servings
Total calories: 2,555

Broiled Duck

I once organized a gastronomic tour of Normandy for my friends the Arakawas. They came back raving about the duck breasts they had eaten. Could I make them duck that tasted that way? No, I said, duck was not for a lady on a diet. Duck was fattening. Duck was too high in calories. Duck fat was bad for your health. But then I would start telling them all the marvelous ways to cook duck, giving them mouth-watering recipes and feeling very sorry for myself for not being able to put into practice all these great recipes. One day a package arrived from a nearby butcher and out of it came the ugliest bird I had ever seen. A duck with no skin. Madeline Arakawa felt that if I liked duck so much and if what was fattening in a duck was its skin, how about a duck with no skin? What could I do with it? My husband suggested broiling. I marinated the duck, broiled it, and served a most delicious bird, which Madeline asserted tasted very much like her Normandy ducks. Maybe it did. I am not so sure, but you should try the recipe. Ask the butcher to remove the skin for you with all its fat and then to cut the duck into 4 serving pieces.

> 2 small ducks, all skin and fat removed, quartered
> 1 tablespoon cumin powder
> 1 tablespoon wine vinegar
> 2 large garlic cloves, crushed
> juice of 2 limes
> 1 tablespoon dried thyme
> salt and pepper
> parsley for garnish
> 1 lemon for garnish

Place the ducks in a bowl. Mix all the other ingredients together, add to the bowl, coat the ducks well with the mixture, and refrigerate for 2 hours.

Preheat the broiler.

Broil the ducks for 10 minutes, about 4 inches from the heat, then turn them over and broil for another 10 minutes, or until the flesh is easily pierced with a fork.

Serve garnished with parsley and lemon wedges.

Yield: 8 servings
Total calories: 3,420

Hot Rabbit and Chicory Salad

This salad was one of my father's favorites. Instead of using oil, he used excellent bacon fat or goose fat. Very fattening! I adapted his recipe using a little olive oil instead. Use a good strong French-style mustard in the dressing. This dish is a meal in itself. With it you can indulge in eating a fresh Italian bread and serve a good dessert.

> 1 fresh rabbit, cut into serving pieces (about 3 pounds
>   ready to cook)
> 1 tablespoon olive oil
> 3 hot green peppers, chopped
> 1 cup hot water
> 2 heads chicory
> 2 teaspoons strong Dijon mustard
> 1 garlic clove, mashed
> 2 teaspoons wine vinegar
> salt and pepper
> chopped chives for garnish

Preheat the oven to 475°.

Place the rabbit in a baking pan and brush all the pieces with some of the oil. Sprinkle with the chopped hot peppers. Bake in the 475° oven for 15 minutes. Then turn the rabbit pieces over, brush again with the remaining oil, and cook for another 30 minutes at 450°.

Remove the rabbit to a bowl to cool. Pour 1 cup of hot water into the baking pan, and scrape the sides and bottom of the pan. Heat until reduced to ½ cup and set aside.

Wash the chicory. Discard any tough leaves; use just the light green and yellow leaves. Put the leaves in a large salad bowl.

Remove the rabbit meat from the bones and cut it into narrow strips 2 inches long. Add the rabbit to the reduced pan juices.

In a bowl, mix together the Dijon mustard, garlic, and vinegar, and add 2 tablespoons of the rabbit juice. Correct the seasoning with salt and pepper. Add to the salad and toss well.

Gently heat the rabbit in its juice. Add to the salad and toss gently. Serve sprinkled with chopped chives.

Yield: 6 servings
Total calories: 1,795

Rabbit Terrine with Vegetables

Rabbits are readily available in supermarkets. They are often frozen, from Canada. To make a terrine, you do not have to have a fresh rabbit.

> *1 quart chicken bouillon*
> *1 rabbit, cut into small serving pieces (about 3 pounds*
> > *ready to cook)*
> *1 tablespoon coriander seeds*
> *salt and pepper*
> *4 small carrots*
> *1 eggplant*
> *2 zucchini*
> *1 bunch broccoli*
> *3 medium-size tomatoes*
> *½ pound fresh peas in their shells*
> *½ pound small onions*
> *2 kohlrabi*
> *2 tablespoons olive oil*
> *2 tablespoons dried tarragon*
> *3 envelopes unflavored gelatin*
> *3 tablespoons cold water*
> *parsley for garnish*
>
> *2-quart mold*

In a large saucepan bring the chicken bouillon to a boil. Add the rabbit, coriander seeds, and salt and pepper, lower the heat, and simmer for 1 hour.

Dice the carrots. Peel and dice the eggplant. Wash and dice the zucchini. Wash the broccoli and cut it into very small florets; discard the stems. Peel the tomatoes, quarter and seed, then dice. Shell the peas. Peel the onions. Peel and dice the kohlrabi.

In a large skillet heat the oil, then add all the vegetables, and sauté for a few minutes until golden brown. Then add 1 cup of the rabbit bouillon. Add salt and pepper and the tarragon. Cook over very high heat until most of the liquid has evaporated.

With a slotted spoon remove the rabbit to a bowl and cool.

Strain the bouillon and add more chicken bouillon, or water, to measure 4¼ cups. In a small bowl soak the gelatin in 3 table-spoons of cold water, then add the gelatin to the bouillon, and heat until it is completely dissolved. Pour some gelatin in the bottom of the mold and refrigerate until it sets. Then decorate with some parsley, pour in more gelatin, and refrigerate again.

Meanwhile, remove the meat from the rabbit bones.

Put a layer of vegetables in the bottom of the mold, then a layer of rabbit, then a layer of vegetables, then rabbit—until all the ingredients are used. Pour the remaining gelatin over all and refrigerate for a day.

Serve sliced, with a light sauce such as Fresh Tomato Sauce (page 225).

Yield: 8 to 10 servings
Total calories: 2,945

Rabbit with Ginger

Two blocks down from my house in Manhattan is the last of New York's live poultry markets. It is a wide store full of cages filled with chickens, hens, and rabbits. The owner, an enormous man, sits outside the store smoking his cigarette, waiting for his customers. He will sell you fresh eggs if he likes you. He always refuses to talk to me if I buy a chicken, but if I am asking for rabbits, we then have a little chat before he selects two for me. We have often exchanged recipes. His rabbit recipes are full of garlic or they are stewed in wine. The following recipe is a compromise between his recipe, mine, and my grandmother's.

2 small rabbits, or 1 medium-size one (about 2 pounds in
*   all, ready to cook)*
1 tablespoon soy sauce
2-inch piece fresh ginger
2 garlic cloves
salt and pepper
2 tablespoons dried rosemary
juice of 1 lemon
1 cup dry white wine
1 cup chicken bouillon
watercress or parsley for garnish

Preheat the oven to 375°.

Wipe the rabbit and rub with soy sauce. Peel the ginger and the garlic and chop fine together. Rub the mixture on the rabbit. Sprinkle with salt, pepper, rosemary, and lemon juice.

Place the rabbit in an ovenproof pan, pour over it the wine and the bouillon, and bake in the 375° oven for 1 hour, basting *very often*. (As you are using no fats and because rabbit is dry, it is important to baste it.)

When the rabbit is done (test it with a fork), carve it into several serving pieces. Pour the pan juices over it, garnish with watercress or parsley, and serve with steamed potatoes.

Yield: 4 servings
Total calories: 1,250

VEAL, LAMB & BEEF

Blanquette de Veau à la Vapeur

My mother's only masterpiece! She cooked this blanquette by mistake, having misread my recipe. Her blanquette turned out to be so delicious that it became her most favorite recipe.

1 celery stalk, cut in 1-inch pieces
5 parsley sprigs
2 thyme sprigs
2 bay leaves
2 pounds breast of veal, cut into 2-inch pieces
3 cloves
salt and pepper
8 small onions + 1 medium onion
8 large white mushrooms
2 turnips
2 carrots
2 egg yolks
3½ ounces low-fat farmer's cheese
2 lemons

2 steamer racks and 1 lid

Cut the celery into 1-inch pieces. Line 1 steamer rack with the celery, parsley, thyme, and bay leaves. Spread the veal on top. Add the cloves and sprinkle with salt and pepper.

Steam the veal, covered, for 40 minutes in all, or until it is tender. Peel the 8 small onions and trim and wipe the mushrooms. Ten minutes before the meat is done, add the onions to the steamer, and 5 minutes before the meat is done, add the mushrooms.

Meanwhile, make the sauce. Scrape the carrots. Peel the turnips and remaining onion. Put the vegetables in the second steamer rack, stack on top of the first rack, cover, and steam for 15 minutes. In a food processor place the carrots, turnips, onion, egg yolks, cheese, and the juice of 1 lemon. Run the machine until all the ingredients are puréed. Remove the purée to a saucepan and add salt and pepper and more lemon juice to taste. (Add up to ½ cup water to thin the sauce if it is too thick.)

Transfer the veal, onions, and mushrooms from their steamer rack to a large serving bowl. Discard the celery, parsley, thyme and bay leaves. Pour the sauce over all and serve.

Yield: 6 servings
Total calories: 2,580

Steamed Veal with Sage and Gooseberries

Gooseberries remind me of English nursery rhymes that my mother-in-law used to sing to my children or tales of jams being made in the spring in a country kitchen. Today gooseberries are reappearing in the markets. They are either green or green streaked with red. When ripe, they are excellent with white meats such as veal or chicken. If you cannot find gooseberries, replace them with sour cherries, whose tart taste will work well with the sweetness of veal.

2 pounds veal (taken from the leg), cut into 1-inch cubes
2 limes
1 tablespoon wine vinegar
2 tablespoons dried thyme
salt and pepper
4 Boston lettuce leaves
3 fresh sage leaves
1 pint red gooseberries or pitted sour cherries
1 bunch parsley
1 bunch watercress
½ cup chicken bouillon

Marinate the veal. Place the meat in a bowl, add the juice of 1 lime and the wine vinegar, thyme, and salt and pepper. Mix well, cover, and refrigerate for 2 hours.

Just before dinner, line a steamer with the lettuce leaves, place the veal on top, then the sage leaves. Cover and steam for 6 minutes. Then add the gooseberries or cherries. Steam for 1 minute more. Remove to a heated platter.

Wash, drain and dry the parsley and watercress. Cut off and discard their stems. In a food processor or blender, purée them together with the bouillon. Pour into a saucepan and heat slowly. Cook for 5 minutes. Correct the seasoning with salt, pepper, and lime juice from the remaining lime. Transfer to a sauceboat. Serve the veal with Steamed Okra with Earmushrooms (page 192).

Yield: 6 servings
Total calories: 1,270

Charcoal-Broiled Veal Burgers with Mustard Sauce

1½ pounds ground veal
1½ cups yogurt
½ teaspoon cumin
salt and pepper
1 teaspoon Dijon mustard
¼ teaspoon ground ginger
1 tablespoon lime juice
watercress for garnish

Have the butcher grind the veal. Mix it with ½ cup of the yogurt, the cumin, and salt and pepper. Shape into 4 patties, and broil over a charcoal fire until brown on both sides. Meanwhile make the sauce. Mix together the remaining yogurt and the mustard, ginger, and lime juice. Remove the broiled patties to a platter, garnish with watercress, and serve the sauce from a sauceboat.

Yield: 4 servings
Total calories: 1,250

Variation on Veal Burgers

6 large Chinese dried mushrooms
1 cup hot water
1½ pounds ground veal
½ cup yogurt
1 garlic clove, chopped
¼ teaspoon cumin
salt and pepper
1 tablespoon black soy sauce (see page 11)
parsley for garnish
1 cup fresh red currants for garnish

Have the butcher grind the veal. Soak the Chinese mushrooms for ½ hour in 1 cup of hot water. Meanwhile in a bowl, mix together the veal, yogurt, garlic, cumin, and pepper to taste. Set aside.

Drain the mushrooms and reserve the mushroom water. Remove the mushroom stems. Chop 3 mushrooms coarsely and add them to the veal. Mix well and make 4 flat patties.

Heat a frying pan with ½ tablespoon salt. When it is hot, add the veal patties and brown on both sides over medium heat. Then add ½ cup of the mushroom water, the remaining mushrooms, and the soy sauce. Cook over medium heat for 8 minutes.

Serve garnished with parsley and the red currants and with steamed summer squash.

Yield: 4 servings
Total calories: 1,535

Medallion of Veal on a Bed of String Beans

When I first came to the United States, veal as I used to have in France, milk-fed, white or pale pink, was difficult to find. In fact, I was rarely served veal unless I went to an Italian restaurant. Today things have changed. Veal, quite expensive, is probably the best quality meat one can get in the United States. Paul Bocuse, the French chef, told me that when he comes to this country he always takes back with him Plume de Veau veal, which he considers the best veal, better than in France. Most veal dishes taste infinitely better if the veal used is of good quality, pale in color and with no fat. In this recipe I used the filet mignon of veal cut 1½ inches thick and quickly cooked. The meat is tender and exquisite.

2 pounds small thin string beans
1 lemon
¼ teaspoon sugar
3 tablespoons cold water
2 tablespoons butter
4 filets mignons of veal, 1½ to 2 inches thick
salt and pepper
1 cup chicken bouillon
1 tablespoon soy sauce
2 tablespoons chopped parsley for garnish

Snap off the ends of the string beans. Wash and drain. Place the string beans in a steamer and wait until the meat is done to steam them.

Wash the lemon, remove the zest, and cut it into a very fine julienne. Place in a small saucepan, cover with cold water, and bring to a boil. Then drain immediately and rinse under cold water. Put the zest back in the saucepan, add the sugar and 3 tablespoons of cold water, and boil over medium heat until all the water has evaporated. Set aside.

In a skillet heat the butter, add the filets mignons, and cook for 5 minutes over high heat. Add salt and pepper, then turn over and cook for another 5 minutes. Remove to a heated platter and keep warm.

Steam the string beans, covered, for 5 minutes. While they are cooking, discard the butter in the skillet and add the bouillon and the lemon zest. Cook over medium heat, scraping the skillet, and reduce the bouillon by half. Add the soy sauce and salt and pepper to taste.

Place the beans on a large platter, and place the veal on top of the beans. Pour the sauce over the veal, sprinkle with chopped parsley, and serve.

Yield: 4 servings
Total calories: 2,195

Filets Mignons of Veal with Mustard

This is a very elegant dish. Have the butcher slice the filet mignon about 2½ inches thick. The veal is cooked with old-fashioned French mustard, which means the mustard seeds are still whole, not ground. The meat should be marinated the night before.

1½ cups dry white wine
2 tablespoons old-fashioned French mustard
1 small can tomato paste
20 coriander seeds
6 filets mignons of veal, about 2½ inches thick
1 pound white mushrooms
6 shallots, chopped
¼ cup chopped parsley
salt and pepper
juice of 1 lemon
parsley for garnish

In a bowl large enough to hold the meat, mix together the white wine, mustard, tomato paste, and coriander seeds. Add the meat and refrigerate for 24 hours, turning the meat once or twice.

Wash, pat dry, and trim the mushrooms. In a saucepan mix together the mushrooms, shallots, parsley, salt and pepper, and lemon juice. Cook over low heat, covered, for 10 minutes. Correct the seasoning.

Place the meat in a large saucepan and add the mushroom mixture and the marinade. Bring to a boil, lower the heat, and simmer for 30 minutes. Remove the meat, arrange on a serving platter, and keep warm.

Simmer the cooking liquid until reduced by half. Pour this sauce over the meat, garnish with chopped parsley, and serve.

Yield: 6 servings
Total calories: 2,785

Veal Roast with Orange and Lemon

2 large garlic cloves
3½-pound boneless veal roast
3 tablespoons butter
¼ cup brandy
1 cup chicken bouillon
1 tablespoon wine vinegar
1 tablespoon chopped fresh thyme
salt and pepper
4 oranges
1 lemon
parsley for garnish

Peel and sliver the garlic. With a pointed knife make deep holes in the veal and insert the garlic in them. In a large heavy saucepan heat the butter. When it is hot, add the veal and brown on all sides. Pour in the brandy and ignite. When the flames die down, add the chicken bouillon, wine vinegar, thyme, and salt and pepper. Simmer for 1 hour.

Meanwhile carefully peel off the zests of the oranges and the lemon. Cut all zests into fine julienne strips. Squeeze the oranges and lemon and add the juice to the veal. When the veal is cooked, remove to a platter and keep warm.

Reduce the cooking liquid by half by cooking it over high heat. Correct the seasoning and add the orange and lemon zests. Slice the veal, cover with the reduced sauce, and garnish with parsley.

Yield: 6 to 8 servings
Total calories: 2,945

Veal Stuffed with Shrimp

6 large veal scallops (about 3 pounds)
¾ pound small shrimp in their shells
2 cups water
salt

2 garlic cloves
¼ pound shallots
¾ cup parsley leaves
3 tablespoons chopped chives
3 eggs
pepper
1 teaspoon paprika
3 cups chicken bouillon
parsley or watercress for garnish

Have the butcher pound the veal scallops so that they are quite thin and large enough to hold the stuffing.

Preheat the oven to 450°.

Peel the shrimp, cook them in 2 cups of boiling salted water for 5 minutes, and drain immediately. Wash and pat dry the parsley. Remove the stems. Peel the shallots and garlic. Chop the shrimp together with the shallots, garlic, parsley, and chives in a food processor or with a large sharp knife.

Heat a non-stick skillet and scramble the eggs until they are just done but still quite soft. Remove from the heat and add the chopped shrimp. Mix well and correct the seasoning with salt and pepper.

Prepare 6 squares of foil each big enough to hold 1 roll of the stuffed veal. In the center of the foil place the veal scallop, sprinkle with paprika, place some stuffing in the center, and roll the scallop to enclose the stuffing. Then roll the foil paper and twist the ends so that no liquid will get to the veal.

Place the 6 veal rolls in a gratin dish large enough to hold them in 1 layer. Pour the bouillon over them and bake in the 450° oven for 20 minutes.

To serve, remove the foil from the rolls in a serving platter and pour ½ cup of the cooking bouillon over them. Garnish with parsley or watercress.

Yield: 6 servings
Total calories: 2,795

Sweetbread and Kidney Brochette

1 pair veal sweetbreads (about 1 pound)
2 veal kidneys (about 1 pound)
1 quart water
1 tablespoon coarse salt
pepper
1 pint cherry tomatoes
1 tablespoon olive oil
2 tablespoons finely chopped fresh rosemary
2 pounds long Chinese string beans or regular string beans
1 cup yogurt
juice of ½ lemon
½ teaspoon cumin
2 tablespoons chopped chives

6 skewers for broiling

Wash the sweetbreads and soak for 1 hour. Wash the kidneys and soak for 1 hour. Drain the sweetbreads and kidneys and pat dry.

In a large saucepan, bring 1 quart of water to a boil. Add ½ tablespoon coarse salt and some pepper. Add the sweetbreads, bring back to a boil, then lower the heat, and simmer for 10 minutes. Drain and cool. Remove the skin and sinews. Cut the kidneys in two lengthwise. Remove the central core and the skin. Cut both the kidneys and the sweetbreads into slices 2 inches thick.

On each skewer place first a tomato, then a piece of sweetbread, a piece of kidney, a second tomato, then sweetbread and kidney again, and end with a tomato. Do the same to all the skewers. Sprinkle with salt and pepper. Brush with the olive oil and roll in the rosemary.

Broil the skewers for 6 to 7 minutes, turning them often. At the same time, steam the string beans, covered, for 6 or 7 minutes. Place the beans on a long serving platter. Sprinkle with salt and pepper, then place the 6 skewers on top.

Mix together the yogurt, lemon, and cumin, add the chives, mix well, and serve with the meat.

Yield: 6 servings
Total calories: 2,155

Sweetbreads with Chinese Okra and Bok Choy (Chinese Cabbage)

Chinese okra looks like a large cucumber, about 6 inches to 7 inches long, with tough ridges on all its length. Be sure to remove the ridges before cooking the okra. As for the Chinese cabbage or *bok choy*, it has large, dark green leaves with thick white stems. Each cabbage has about 10 leaves or more. Allow ½ a cabbage per person.

> *3 Chinese okra*
> *2 Chinese cabbages*
> *1 pair veal sweetbreads (about 1 pound)*
> *1 teaspoon salt*
> *1 tablespoon butter*
> *pepper*
> *nutmeg*
> *2-inch piece fresh ginger, grated*
> *1 soft bean curd cake*
> *1 cup yogurt*
> *2 egg yolks*
> *2 tablespoons soy sauce*

Wash the Chinese okra and cut into 1-inch pieces after having removed all the ridges. Set aside. Wash the *bok choy* and cut them in two lengthwise. Wash the sweetbreads and soak for 1 hour.

Place the drained sweetbreads in a large saucepan, cover with cold water, and add 1 teaspoon salt and pepper. Bring to a boil, then lower the heat, and simmer for 6 minutes. Drain and cool under cold running water. Remove any sinews and skin. Cut the sweetbreads into slices ½ inch thick.

Preheat the oven to 450°.

In a skillet heat the butter, add the sweetbreads, and sauté for 5 minutes. Sprinkle with salt and pepper, nutmeg, and ginger. Cover and keep warm while cooking the vegetables.

Steam the okra and cabbage together, covered, for 5 minutes. Remove to a plate.

In a food processor place the bean curd, yogurt, egg yolks, salt and pepper, and the soy sauce. Run the machine until all the ingredients are puréed.

Line a baking pan with the vegetables, pour some of the bean-curd sauce over them, arrange the slices of sweetbreads on top, and cover with the remaining sauce. Bake in the 450° oven until the top is golden brown. Serve right away.

Yield: 4 servings
Total calories: 1,835

Sweetbread and Arugola Salad

Arugola is an Italian salad, slightly bitter, with leaves that resemble large watercress leaves. Sweetbreads mixed with them make an excellent lunch or a light main course for a summer evening.

1 pair veal sweetbreads (about 1 pound)
1 tablespoon light soy sauce
salt and pepper
juice of 1 lemon
1 tablespoon chopped fresh chives
½ pound arugola

Wash the sweetbreads several times under cold running water. Steam them, covered, for 5 minutes and remove to a bowl to cool.

Remove the membranes and cut the sweetbreads into thin slices. In a saucepan place the soy sauce and the slices of sweetbread and sauté for 5 minutes. Correct the seasoning with salt and pepper and remove to a bowl. Add the lemon juice and chives and set aside. Wash and pat dry the arugola.

Mix salad with the sweetbreads, toss well, and refrigerate until ready to serve.

Yield: 4 servings
Total calories: 1,015

Roast Baby Leg of Lamb with Small Artichokes

In the spring, small artichokes arrive in the market. They are Italian artichokes. Baked with a leg of lamb, they add a wonderful flavor to the roast.

   16 very small artichokes
   1 lemon
   4- to 5-pound leg of spring lamb
   3 large garlic cloves
   salt and pepper
   2 tablespoons dried sage
   2 cups chicken bouillon
   1 tablespoon soy sauce
   parsley for garnish

Preheat the oven to 425°.

Slice off the stems of the artichokes. With a sharp knife, cut off about 1 inch from the tops. With a coffee spoon, remove the center choke. Place the artichokes in a bowl of water. Cut the lemon in two, squeeze some of the juice into the water, and add the lemon halves to the water. This will prevent the artichokes from turning brown.

Cut most of the fat off the leg of lamb, or have the butcher do it. Peel and slice the garlic. Make several incisions in the leg of lamb and insert the pieces of garlic. Sprinkle the leg with salt and pepper, place it on a rack in a roasting pan, and sprinkle with the sage. Add the bouillon and place the drained artichokes around the lamb. Bake in the 425° oven for 1½ hours (or to an internal temperature of 135° to 140°) if you like it medium rare. Baste frequently.

Remove the leg from the pan. Slice thin and arrange on a heated serving platter. Remove the artichokes and arrange around the lamb. Degrease the pan juices, correct the seasoning by adding soy sauce, mix well, and serve in a sauceboat. Garnish the platter with parsley.

Yield: 6 to 8 servings
Total calories: 3,860

Herbed Leg of Lamb with Paprika

A few summers ago a friend and I went on a nostalgic tour of Hungary, her grandparents having come from there. We met several of her relatives in Budapest. One of them invited us to their house for dinner and served us this delicious leg of lamb. The recipe calls for fresh herbs. If they are not available, try it with dried ones. The result is good, but it's superb if they are fresh.

6½- to 7-pound leg of lamb
2 tablespoons vegetable oil
1 teaspoon chopped fresh thyme
1 teaspoon chopped fresh sage
1 tablespoon chopped fresh rosemary
few drops Tabasco
1 teaspoon paprika
salt and pepper
2 cups water
4 carrots, chopped
4 celery stalks, chopped
2 leeks, cleaned and chopped
2 medium-size onions, chopped
2 sweet red peppers, seeded and chopped

Ask the butcher to remove all the fat from the leg of lamb.

Preheat the oven to 475°.

In a bowl place the oil, add the herbs, Tabasco, and paprika, and mix well. Rub the leg of lamb with this mixture and sprinkle it with salt and pepper.

Heat 2 cups of water, place the lamb in a roasting pan, and pour the hot water over it. Roast for 1½ hours in the 475° oven (or to an internal temperature of 135° to 140° for medium rare), basting from time to time.

Half an hour before the end of cooking, add all the vegetables to the pan. When the lamb is cooked the vegetables should be just barely done. Serve the leg of lamb surrounded by the vegetables and with small steamed potatoes.

Yield: 8 to 10 servings
Total calories: 5,600

Pot-au-Feu en Gelée

5 pounds brisket of beef (all fat removed) + some soup
        bones
2 large garlic cloves
about 2 quarts water
1 onion stuck with 2 cloves
1 bay leaf
2 tablespoons dried thyme
10 peppercorns
coarse salt
1 leek
2 celery stalks
6 carrots
4 tomatoes
15 cornichons (sour gherkins) + extras for garnish
3 envelopes unflavored gelatin
½ tablespoon soy sauce
chopped parsley for garnish
2 cups Parsley Sauce (page 224)

2-quart mold

Wash the soup bones. Make several incisions in the meat. Cut the garlic in slivers and insert into the meat. In a large soup kettle place the bones and the meat. Cover with water (about 2 quarts), bring to a boil, lower the heat, and skim the surface several times. Then add the onion, bay leaf, thyme, peppercorns, and coarse salt. Meanwhile scrape and wash the carrots and trim and wash the leek and celery. Slice 2 of the carrots. Cut the remaining carrots and the leek and celery into 2-inch pieces.

After the meat has cooked for 1 hour, add the vegetables to the soup and cook for another 1½ hours or until the meat is tender when pierced with a fork. Remove the meat from the soup to a platter, cool, then refrigerate for 1 hour. Strain the bouillon and refrigerate for 1 hour. The fat then rises to the surface and can be easily removed.

Set aside the sliced carrots. Peel the tomatoes and cut them into 2-inch slices. Set aside. Slice the *cornichons.*

In a small bowl soak the gelatin in 2 tablespoons of water. Into a saucepan pour 1 cup of beef bouillon, heat, then add the gelatin and stir over low heat until it is totally dissolved. Add 3¼ cups of the remaining bouillon and add ½ tablespoon soy sauce. Correct the seasoning.

Pour some gelatin-bouillon mixture in the bottom of the mold. Garnish with parsley and place in the freezer for 10 minutes. Meanwhile slice the meat.

Fill the mold with layers of the sliced meat alternating layers with slices of carrots, tomatoes, and *cornichons* until all the meat has been used. Cover with the remaining bouillon and refrigerate overnight.

Dip the bottom of the mold in hot water, unmold onto a round platter, and garnish with extra *cornichons* and parsley. Serve with Parsley Sauce.

Yield: 8 servings
Total calories: 4,430

Hamburgers with Braised Finocchi

Finocchi have that marvelous anise flavor and are crunchy and crisp when eaten raw. Barely cooked, served with lean broiled hamburgers, they add something unusual to an ordinary dish.

4 finocchi *bulbs (fennel)*
¼ *cup strong chicken bouillon*
1 *tablespoon soy sauce*
few drops Oriental hot oil
1 *tablespoon sugar*
salt and pepper
4 *lean broiled hamburgers (about 1½ pounds in all)*
chopped parsley for garnish

Cut off the stems of the *finocchi*. Cut the *finocchi* into julienne strips with the slicing blade of a food processor. Or, with a sharp knife, cut them first in two lengthwise and cut each piece in two again. Then slice thin.

In a saucepan, place the bouillon, soy sauce, and the hot oil. Add the julienned *finocchi*, sugar, and salt and pepper to taste. Bring to a boil and boil, uncovered, for 5 minutes. Remove to a serving platter, place broiled hamburgers on top, and sprinkle with chopped parsley.

Yield: 4 servings
Total calories: 1,290

PASTA, RICE & BUCKWHEAT

Spaghetti with Fresh Tomatoes

Spaghetti and fresh pasta have always brought to my mind images of pounds being added to my waistline. I would watch enviously my son Thomas (who has always said that he is an Italian at heart) eating mounds of spaghetti. Now that I have discovered that 1 pound of spaghetti can be stretched to only 280 calories per portion, I have had a wonderful time experimenting with different sauces. My main problem has been to convince him that my sauces are as good as his favorite Bolognese sauce. After several tries, I brought him over to my camp and claimed victory.

The best way to make this sauce is to use fresh plum tomatoes. If the tomatoes are not in season, use canned plum tomatoes.

> *1 pound fresh plum tomatoes, or a 1-pound can plum*
> *   tomatoes*
> *½ cup coarsely chopped fresh basil leaves*
> *2 garlic cloves, chopped*
> *3 tablespoons* pignoli *nuts*
> *juice of ½ lime*
> *1 tablespoon very good olive oil*
> *salt and pepper*
> *1 pound spaghetti*
> *¼ cup grated Parmesan (optional)*

Plunge the fresh tomatoes into 1 quart of boiling water and turn off the heat. Let them stand in the hot water for 5 minutes, then drain and refresh under cold running water. Peel the tomatoes, cut into 3 or 4 pieces, and seed. (If using canned tomatoes, just drain them.)

Heat 2 quarts water in a large kettle, adding 1 tablespoon salt. When the water boils, add the spaghetti.

In a saucepan place the tomatoes and add the basil, garlic, and *pignoli* nuts. Add the lime juice, oil, and salt and pepper to taste, mix carefully, and heat slowly. Do not cook the tomatoes. When the spaghetti is cooked, drain well and serve with the sauce on the side. Grated Parmesan can be added.

Yield: 6 servings
Total calories: 2,190

Spaghetti with Spinach and Chinese Mushrooms

This dish is very quick to make as the sauce can be done while the water for the spaghetti is being heated. The water in which the mushrooms have soaked is used to extend the sauce and moisten the spaghetti.

10 Chinese dried mushrooms
2 pieces "black fungus" (optional; see Note)
2 cups hot water
2 garlic cloves
1 pound thin spaghetti
1 pound fresh spinach
1 tablespoon olive oil
salt and pepper
2 ounces grated Parmesan

Soak the Chinese mushrooms and the black fungus seaweed in the hot water for 20 minutes. Drain and reserve the water. Remove the stems of the mushrooms and cut the mushrooms and seaweed into julienne strips. Peel the garlic and chop.

Heat 3 quarts of water, adding 1 tablespoon salt. When the water boils, add the spaghetti.

Wash and trim the spinach, pat dry, and cut the leaves into narrow strips. In a large skillet heat the olive oil, add the chopped garlic, and sauté for a few seconds. Then add the mushrooms and the black fungus and sauté for 5 minutes over medium heat. Add the spinach, sauté for a few seconds, mix well, and add salt and pepper. Add ½ cup of the mushroom water and heat thoroughly.

When the spaghetti is cooked, drain well and place in a bowl. Pour the spinach sauce on top and mix at the table. Serve the grated Parmesan alongside.

Yield: 4 to 5 servings
Total calories: 2,165

NOTE: "Black fungus" is a seaweed that, when dried, looks like a shriveled black mushroom. After soaking, it opens into a large round seaweed with scalloped edges. It is an excellent seasoning and can be found in all oriental food stores and in most health-food stores that carry a good range of natural spices.

Pasta Shells with Zucchini

4 small zucchini
2 tablespoons olive oil
3 garlic cloves, sliced
salt and pepper
1 cup dry white wine
2 tablespoons chopped parsley
1-pound pasta shells
2 ounces grated Parmesan

Wash the zucchini and slice thin. In a skillet, heat the oil, add the zucchini and sliced garlic, and sauté for 4 minutes. Sprinkle with salt and pepper and add the white wine and chopped parsley. Cover and simmer for 10 minutes.

Meanwhile heat 2 quarts of water with 1 teaspoon salt. When the water boils, add the shells and cook, uncovered, for 12 minutes or until they are done. Drain and put in a large bowl. Pour the zucchini with their juice over the shells. Serve grated Parmesan alongside.

Yield: 4 servings
Total calories: 2,275

Capellini with Smoked Salmon, Capers and Mushrooms

Capellini are very thin pasta, very light, and quick to cook. They can be eaten cold in a salad or hot with any sauce you like. Here the sauce is colorful—smoked salmon with Chinese mushrooms and capers.

6 shiitake mushrooms
½ cup water
salt and pepper
2 tablespoons capers

1 *pound* capellini
¼ *pound sliced smoked salmon, cut in 1 inch pieces*
chopped parsley for garnish

Soak the *shiitake* mushrooms in ½ cup cold water for 1 hour. Drain the mushrooms, reserving the liquid. Remove the mushroom stems and slice the caps thin. Heat the mushroom liquid. When it boils, add the mushrooms and cook for 10 minutes. Add salt and pepper to taste. Turn off the heat and add the capers.

In a large kettle bring 2 quarts of water to boil with 1 tablespoon salt. Add the pasta and cook for 5 minutes or until the *capellini* are cooked. Drain immediately. Place the *capellini* in a bowl, add the *shiitake* mushrooms and their liquid and the smoked salmon, mix well, and sprinkle with the chopped parsley. Serve immediately.

Yield: 4 servings
Total calories: 1,920

Rice Noodles with Bay Scallops

Rice noodles are sold either fresh or dried. When they are dry, they are a yellowish-white color. They are sold in 1-pound bags and are called rice sticks in Chinatown. To prepare the dry noodles, put in a bowl, cover with water, and leave to soak for 10 to 15 minutes until they are supple and can be easily handled. When fresh, they are sold in 1-pound bags and need not be soaked.

½ *pound dry "rice stick" noodles*
2 *tablespoons soy sauce*
½ *pound small bay scallops*
1 *tablespoon lime juice*
1-*inch piece fresh ginger, grated*
salt and pepper
chopped Chinese parsley (coriander)

Prepare the noodles as described above. In a saucepan bring 2 cups of water to a boil, add the noodles, and cook for 4 minutes. Drain, put in a bowl, and add the soy sauce immediately (it prevents them from sticking together).

Wash and pat dry the scallops. Steam them, covered, for 2 minutes. Add the scallops to the noodles with the lime juice, ginger, salt and pepper to taste, and the chopped Chinese parsley. Toss well and serve right away.

Yield: 4 servings
Total calories: 1,045

Fresh Noodles with Blue Cheese Sauce

1 cup yogurt
3½ ounces blue cheese
2 egg yolks
salt and pepper
1 pound fresh noodles

In a large kettle bring to a boil 2 quarts of water with ½ tablespoon salt. While the water is heating make the sauce. In a food processor place the yogurt, the blue cheese cut in small pieces, the egg yolks, and pepper. Run the machine until the mixture is smooth. Remove to a bowl and taste to see if it needs salt.

Plunge the fresh noodles into the boiling water and stir. Cook, stirring occasionally, for 5 minutes after the water starts to boil again, or until the noodles are done. Drain, put in a large bowl, and pour the sauce over them. Toss the noodles and serve.

Yield: 6 servings
Total calories: 2,370

Fresh Pasta with Dried Chinese and Polish Mushrooms

The idea of this simple sauce is to soak the 2 kinds of dried mushrooms and use their water to cook the fresh ones. It is best served on top of fresh pasta. Polish mushrooms have a very strong taste, Chinese mushrooms are more delicate and more tender.

> *2½ cups warm water*
> *1 ounce Polish dried mushrooms*
> *2 ounces Chinese dried mushrooms*
> *1 pound fresh white mushrooms*
> *salt and pepper*
> *2 garlic cloves, chopped*
> *1½ pounds fresh* tagliatelli
> *2 ounces grated Parmesan (optional)*

Soak the Polish mushrooms in 1 cup of warm water for 1 hour or more. Soak the Chinese mushrooms for 1 hour in 1½ cups of warm water.

Wash and pat dry the white mushrooms. Cut off the stems and slice the caps. Set aside. Drain the Chinese and Polish mushrooms, reserving the liquid. (Combine the two liquids.) Remove the stems from the Chinese mushrooms and slice the caps into long thin strips. In a skillet heat 1 cup of the mushroom water. When it starts to boil, add the sliced fresh mushrooms and salt and pepper and the garlic. Reduce the heat and cook for 5 minutes; then add the Chinese mushrooms and the Polish mushrooms. Cook for another 10 minutes, adding some of the water from the soaking. You should always have about ¾ cup liquid in the skillet.

Bring to a boil 2 quarts of water, adding 1 tablespoon salt, for the *tagliatelli*. When the water boils, add the pasta and stir well. When the water comes back to a boil, cook, stirring occasionally, for 4 minutes or until the pasta is done. Drain, place in a large bowl, and pour the mushroom sauce over it. Serve the grated Parmesan alongside.

Yield: 6 servings
Total calories: 2,930

Orzo with Morels

Orzo is a small pasta that looks like rice. In French they are called *langues d'oiseaux*. For years as a small child I would not eat them because our cook had told me jokingly (I was three years old) that these were little birds' tongues, which she had collected for my supper. Today it is one of my favorite dishes. The Italians also have an even smaller pasta, which is called *semi di melone,* melon seeds. These two pastas are easily found in supermarkets or Italian groceries.

> *2 ounces dried morels*
> *½ pound* orzo *or* semi di melone
> *1 tablespoon butter*
> *pepper*

Soak the morels overnight in a bowl of cold water. Drain the morels and reserve the water. Cut them into 2 or 3 pieces, depending on how large they are. In a large saucepan bring 1 quart of water to a boil, adding 1 tablespoon salt. When the water is boiling, add the *orzo* and cook until tender but *al dente.* Drain immediately. Put in a large serving bowl and keep warm.

In a skillet heat the butter, then add the morels and salt and pepper, and sauté for 3 minutes. Add ½ cup of the mushroom water, heat, and pour over the pasta. Toss well and serve.

Yield: 6 servings
Total calories: 1,085

NOTE: *Orzo* is a good substitute for rice, for it has an almost "buttered," slippery texture and needs no butter.

Rice with Black Sesame Seeds

Last fall I was asked to help the artist Miralda celebrate the Thanksgiving festival for animals at the Bronx Zoo. One of my jobs was to prepare a dish for the camel that required several pounds of sesame seeds. When I had finished, I was left with more than a pound of black sesame seeds. For the next few weeks I fed my family dishes sprinkled with them. One of the best was this rice.

> *2 cups long-grain rice*
> *1 tablespoon black sesame seeds*
> *½ tablespoon fennel seeds*
> *salt and pepper*
> *3 cups boiling water*

In a heavy saucepan place the rice and the sesame seeds and mix well. Add the fennel seeds and salt and pepper and mix again. Add the boiling water, bring back to a boil, cover, lower the heat, and cook for 20 minutes, or until all the water has been absorbed. Serve with chicken, fish, or veal.

Yield: 6 servings
Total calories: 1,405

Rice with Lemon Grass and Black Sesame Seeds

> *2 lemon grass stalks (see page 64)*
> *2 cups long-grain rice*
> *1 tablespoon black sesame seeds*
> *salt and pepper*
> *3 cups boiling water*

Wash and trim the lemon grass. Slice very thin. In a saucepan, place the rice, sesame seeds, and lemon grass. Add salt and pepper and mix well. Then add the boiling water, mix again, and cook over very low heat, covered, for 20 minutes, or until all the water has been absorbed.

Serve with roast chicken or broiled lamb.

Yield: 6 servings
Total calories: 1,445

Egyptian Rice with Yogurt

In Cairo my grandmother made this with leftover rice. The rice is crunchy because it is well sautéed in oil before water is added.

FOR THE EGYPTIAN RICE:

1 tablespoon oil
2 cups long-grain rice
2 cups boiling water
1 teaspoon salt
pepper

FOR THE SAUCE:

1 pint yogurt
pepper
1 teaspoon dried mint, crushed

Make the rice. Heat the oil in a heavy-bottomed saucepan. When it is very hot, add the rice and cook over high heat, stirring with a wooden spoon until it turns a golden brown. Add 2 cups of boiling water, 1 teaspoon salt, and pepper. Reduce the heat and cook the rice, covered, for 25 minutes, until all the water is evaporated and the rice is dry. (You may need some more water, but add very little at a time.)

Make the sauce. While the rice is cooking, beat together the yogurt, some pepper, and the mint. Serve the sauce with the rice.

Yield: 6 servings
Total calories: 1,715

Egyptian Rice with Eggplant

3 small eggplants
1 onion
1 tomato
salt and pepper
3 slices ham
1 recipe Egyptian Rice (see preceding recipe)

½ *tablespoon butter for the mold*
1 *tablespoon oil*

1½-*quart* savarin *mold*

Wash and wipe the eggplant. Cut them lengthwise into several slices and set aside the 6 outside slices with skin on 1 side. Dice the remaining slices. Peel and chop the onion. Wash and dice the tomato. Steam these vegetables, covered, for 4 minutes. Remove to a bowl and sprinkle with salt and pepper. Dice the ham and add to the cooked rice.

Butter the *savarin* mold. In a skillet heat the oil and sauté the reserved 6 slices of eggplant, turning them once. Sprinkle with salt and pepper and carefully remove to a platter. Mix the steamed vegetables with the rice and ham and correct the seasoning. Line the mold with the slices of eggplant, skin side down, add the rice mixture, and press down. Unmold onto a round platter and serve.

Yield: 6 servings
Total calories: 2,430

Brown Rice with Steamed Shrimp

1 *tablespoon olive oil*
1 *cup brown rice*
2½ *cups boiling water*
1 *teaspoon salt*
pepper
12 *large shrimp in their shells (about ½ pound)*
2 *tablespoons soy sauce*
2-*inch piece fresh ginger, grated*
½ *teaspoon sesame oil*
2 *tablespoons chopped parsley*
3 *scallions, chopped*
watercress for garnish

In a large saucepan heat the olive oil. When it is hot, add the brown rice and sauté, stirring, until all the rice is coated with the oil. Then add the boiling water, 1 teaspoon salt, and pepper. Mix well, cover tightly, and bring to a boil. Reduce the heat and simmer for 50 minutes or until the rice is tender but not overcooked.

Shell and devein the shrimp. Place them in a steamer and steam, covered, for 4 minutes.

In a small saucepan heat together the soy sauce, ginger, and sesame oil. Add the chopped parsley and scallions and salt and pepper to taste. Put the shrimp in a bowl and pour the sauce over them. Remove the rice to a round serving platter. Put the shrimp on top and pour the sauce over them. Garnish with watercress.

Yield: 4 servings
Total calories: 1,015

Buckwheat with Dill Yogurt

1 cup buckwheat
1 egg, beaten
2 cups chicken bouillon
1 cup yogurt
salt and pepper
3 scallions, chopped
1 tablespoon chopped dill

Place the buckwheat in a bowl, add the egg, and mix well. Heat a large skillet, then add the buckwheat and dry it over medium heat, stirring with a wooden spoon until the grains separate. Add 1½ cups chicken bouillon and bring to a boil. Lower the heat, cover, and cook until all the liquid has been absorbed, about 8 minutes. The buckwheat should be cooked but not too soft. If it is still hard, add the remaining bouillon and continue cooking.

In a bowl beat the yogurt and add some salt and pepper. Add the scallions and the dill. Serve the buckwheat with the yogurt sauce on the side.

Yield: 4 servings
Total calories: 820

VEGETABLES & SALADS

Vegetable Purées

One can imagine very light purées of almost all the colors of the rainbow. And in the winter when vegetables are not as tasty as in the spring, this is a wonderful way to put color into your meals without putting any weight on. The vegetables are puréed with a little cottage cheese or farmer's cheese and served with broiled or roasted meats. All the purées will serve 6.

ORANGE PURÉE:

1½ pounds carrots
2 egg whites
2 tablespoons cottage cheese
coarse salt
pepper
1 tablespoon dried tarragon

Scrape the carrots and cut them into 1-inch pieces. Steam the carrots, covered, for 10 minutes or until tender. Beat the egg whites until stiff and set aside.

In a food processor, place the carrots, cheese, coarse salt, some pepper, and the tarragon. Run the machine until all the ingredients are puréed. Remove to a bowl, gently fold in the egg whites, correct the seasoning, and serve.

Total calories: 360

YELLOW PURÉE:

two 1-pound cans corn kernels
salt
2 tablespoons cottage cheese
pepper

Drain the corn. Place all the ingredients in a food processor and purée. Pour the purée into a saucepan and heat but do not boil. Correct the seasoning and serve.

Total calories: 660

PALE GREEN PURÉE:

1 large cabbage
½ cup cottage cheese
salt and pepper
2 tablespoons chopped parsley

Remove the center core and quarter the cabbage. Steam, covered, for 5 minutes. Remove the cabbage, cut it in pieces, and place cabbage, cheese, and salt and pepper in a food processor. Run the machine until all the ingredients are puréed. Correct the seasoning, add the parsley, and serve.

Total calories: 190

GREEN PURÉE:

6 bunches watercress
3 tablespoons cottage cheese
1 tablespoon dried thyme
1-tablespoon lemon juice
salt and pepper

Wash the watercress, drain, and pat dry. Remove the stems. Steam the watercress, covered, for 3 minutes. Cool and squeeze out all the water.

In a food processor, place the watercress, cheese, and thyme. Run the machine until all the ingredients are puréed. Remove to a saucepan, add the lemon juice, correct the seasoning, and gently heat. Serve immediately.

Total calories: 80

WHITE PURÉE:

2 pounds leeks, white part only
1 celery root
½ cup chicken bouillon
2 tablespoons cottage cheese
1 tablespoon chopped fresh mint
salt and pepper

Trim and wash the leeks and slice thin. Peel the celery root and slice. Steam the celery and leeks, covered, for 8 minutes or until they are done.

In a food processor place the vegetables and the bouillon. Run the machine until all the vegetables are puréed. Pour into a saucepan and add the cheese, mint, and salt and pepper to taste. Simmer for 5 minutes and serve.

Total calories: 295

BROWN PURÉE:

2 pounds white mushrooms
2 ounces dried mushrooms (soak for 1 hour in ½ cup
water)
1 tablespoon cornstarch
2 tablespoons cottage cheese
salt and pepper
pinch of nutmeg

Wash, pat dry, and trim the white mushrooms. Drain the dried mushrooms, reserving the water. Steam the white mushrooms with the dried ones, covered, for 8 minutes.

Remove to a food processor. Add the cornstarch, cottage cheese, reserved mushroom water, salt and pepper, and the nutmeg. Run the machine until all the ingredients are puréed. Pour into a saucepan, heat, correct the seasoning, and serve.

Total calories: 450

Steamed Broccoli and Cauliflower

In the spring the flavor of fresh, young cauliflower is unsurpassed. Sprinkled with fresh parsley and lemon juice, it is a delicious summer vegetable. Add the broccoli and you have two colors. Serve with fresh Carrot Sauce, and you have a superb dish.

1 cauliflower
1 bunch broccoli
salt and pepper
2 tablespoons grated Parmesan
3 tablespoons chopped parsley
juice of 1 lemon
Carrot Sauce (optional)

Remove the cauliflower core. Separate the cauliflower into small florets and place in a steamer. Do the same with the broccoli. Steam, covered, for 6 minutes. Remove to a platter, sprinkle with salt, pepper, and the cheese. Add the parsley and lemon juice.

Yield: 6 servings
Total calories: 325

CARROT SAUCE:

3 carrots
¼ cup chicken bouillon
4 Greek black olives, pitted (optional)
¼ cup chopped fresh basil leaves
salt and pepper
2 tablespoons small capers

Scrape the carrots and cut them into 1-inch pieces. Steam the carrots, covered, for 8 minutes.

In a food processor, place the carrots, bouillon, black olives, basil leaves, and salt and pepper. Run the machine until all the ingredients are puréed. Remove to a bowl, add the capers, and serve with the vegetables.

Yield: 1½ cups
Total calories: 140

Spiced Sautéed Cucumbers

Judy has been traveling to exotic places for many years. Before she leaves on any trip, I always make long speeches to her about paying attention to what she eats and how it is cooked and ask her to bring back recipes she thinks would interest me. This past year on a trip to central Africa, she brought this one, which is strange, but if you try it you will be pleasantly surprised. Serve these cucumbers with drinks or with broiled fish.

2 cucumbers
1 tablespoon oil
1 teaspoon turmeric
1 teaspoon cumin
½ teaspoon black mustard seeds
salt and pepper
3 tablespoons chopped parsley

Peel the cucumbers, cut in two lengthwise, and remove all the seeds with a teaspoon. Cut the cucumbers into strips ¼ inch thick and 2 inches long and set aside.

Heat the oil in a large skillet. Add all the spices. Mix well with a wooden spoon, then brown for a few seconds. Add the cucumbers and sauté for barely 2 minutes, or until they are coated with the spices and hot, *not cooked*. Sprinkle with chopped parsley and serve.

Yield: 4 servings
Total calories: 215

Sugar Snap Peas with Ginger

2 pounds sugar snap peas
2-inch piece fresh ginger
4 scallions
¼ teaspoon sesame oil
2 tablespoons soy sauce
salt and pepper

Trim the snap peas. Peel and slice the ginger. Trim the scallions and cut into 2-inch pieces.

In a food processor put the ginger, scallions, sesame oil, and soy sauce. Run the machine for 1 minute. Pour the mixture into a small saucepan, correct the seasoning, and heat for 1 minute. Set aside.

Five minutes before serving, steam the snap peas, covered. Remove to a serving bowl, pour the sauce over them, and serve right away.

Yield: 4 servings
Total calories: 845

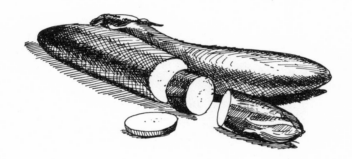

Chinese Eggplant

Chinese eggplant are easily found all year round in Chinese vegetable stores but not as yet in other neighborhoods. If you happen to have a Chinese quarter in your town, explore it. Chinese eggplant are about 6 to 8 inches long, 1½ inches in diameter, and a deep, brilliant purple color. What makes these eggplant so interesting and tasty is that they have a very small center of seeds. They are excellent steamed, baked, or fried.

6 Chinese eggplant
1 cup Parsley Sauce (page 224)
2-inch piece fresh ginger, grated

Cut off the rough ends of each eggplant. Wash them, leave them whole, and steam, covered, for 4 minutes. They will lose their color, but will taste wonderfully good.

Add the grated ginger to the Parsley Sauce and pour it over the eggplant.

Yield: 6 servings
Total calories: 315

Cold Simmered Leeks with Coriander

2 pounds leeks
1 tablespoon olive oil
1 cup dry white wine
1 cup chicken bouillon
15 coriander seeds, crushed
1 bay leaf
3 parsley sprigs
juice of 1 lime
salt and pepper

Cut off the green part of the leeks and discard. Wash the white part and slice thin. In a heavy saucepan heat the oil, add the leeks, and sauté for 2 minutes. Then add the wine, chicken bouillon, coriander seeds, bay leaf, parsley, lime juice, and salt and pepper. Simmer, uncovered, for 45 minutes.

Remove to a bowl and refrigerate until ready to serve. Serve with cold chicken or pâtés.

Yield: 2 cups
Total calories: 445

Steamed Leeks with Coulis of Fresh Tomatoes

1 pound tomatoes
juice of 1 lim
salt and pepper
8 leeks
fresh mint for garnish
1 teaspoon black sesame seeds for garnish

Plunge the tomatoes into boiling water, peel, quarter, and remove all the seeds. Purée the tomatoes in a food processor. Let the purée (*coulis*) stand in the refrigerator for ½ hour and remove the water that will rise to the surface. Add the lime juice and salt and pepper.

Meanwhile, cut the roots off the leeks. Trim the green part but keep most of it, slit the leeks to within 2 inches of the root ends, and wash them under running water to remove the sand. Steam them for 5 minutes, covered. Keep warm.

Arrange the warm leeks in a serving platter. Pour the cold tomato sauce over them, garnish with the fresh mint, and sprinkle with the sesame seeds.

Yield: 4 servings
Total calories: 265

Steamed Turnips with Parsley

8 medium-size turnips
2 bunches parsley
2 garlic cloves
12 black olives, preferably Greek
salt and pepper
½ teaspoon olive oil

Peel the turnips. Cut a slice off one end of each turnip so they can stand up. With a teaspoon make a well at the other end in the center of each turnip. Wash the parsley and pat dry. Peel the garlic. Pit the olives.

In a food processor place the parsley, garlic, and olives. Add salt and pepper. Run the machine until all the ingredients are chopped. Add the olive oil and correct the seasoning.

Fill each cavity with the parsley mixture. Place in a steamer and steam, covered, for 10 minutes.

Serve with broiled chicken.

Yield: 4 servings
Total calories: 600

Braised Turnips with Apple Cider

In this recipe, given to me by my stepfather, a real *normand* from Normandy, the turnips are cooked in French apple cider, which has an alcoholic content similar to that of wine. This type of cider can be found in a good liquor store. The turnips are the first of the season and are small and tender.

> *2 pounds spring turnips*
> *⅓ cup sparkling French apple cider*
> *⅓ cup chicken bouillon*
> *1 tablespoon butter*
> *3 tablespoons chopped parsley*
> *salt and pepper*

Don't peel the spring turnips (though you have to in the winter); wash and scrub them as you would a carrot. In a large saucepan, boil 4 cups of water, add the turnips, bring back to a boil, and cook for 5 minutes. Drain immediately and pat dry with paper towels.

In a saucepan bring the cider to the boiling point. Add the chicken bouillon and heat. In a large saucepan, melt the butter, add the turnips, and brown them on all sides. Add the bouillon-cider mixture and the chopped parsley and salt and pepper. Cover and simmer for 15 minutes.

Serve with broiled Veal Burgers (page 153).

Yield: 4 servings
Total calories: 350

Turnips with Dill Mayonnaise

8 turnips
2 egg yolks
½ cup low-fat yogurt
juice of ½ lemon
salt and pepper
1 tablespoon chopped dill

Peel the turnips and steam, covered, for 10 minutes.
Meanwhile, make the mayonnaise. In a food processor, place the egg yolks and run the machine until they are thick and light in color. Then slowly add the yogurt. When the mayonnaise is thick, add the lemon juice, salt and pepper, and the chopped dill.
Serve the hot turnips in a bowl with the cold mayonnaise on the side.

Yield: 4 servings
Total calories: 580

Boiled Artichokes with Fresh Tomato Sauce

This sauce is wonderful with chicken or fish but I mainly thought of it to serve with boiled artichokes. Juliette, my daughter, always on a diet, loves artichokes but will not eat them with a vinaigrette, so I came up with this sauce for her. It does have olives, but only a few are needed. They should be Greek black olives to give the sauce its particular flavor.

4 large artichokes
1 tablespoon coarse salt
3 ripe tomatoes
6 Greek black olives
salt and pepper
juice of 1 lime
fresh tarragon or basil or oregano (any herb fresh in
*   season), chopped*
Fresh Tomato Sauce (page 225)

In a large kettle place the artichokes, cover with water, add 1 tablespoon coarse salt and bring to a boil. Then lower the heat and simmer for 25 minutes or until the artichoke leaves can be pulled off easily. Drain and cool.

Dip the tomatoes in boiling water, then peel, quarter, and seed them. Remove the pits from the black olives. In a food processor, place the tomatoes, olives, salt and pepper, and the lime juice. Run the machine, using the stop-and-go method, so that the tomatoes are chopped fine but not puréed. Remove to a bowl and add the fresh herb. Correct the seasoning.

Cut off the stems of the artichokes. Push aside the outside leaves and remove the center leaves all at once. Set aside. With a teaspoon remove the chokes. In the center of each artichoke place some tomato sauce, then place the center leaves upside down in the artichokes.

Serve lukewarm with the remaining cold sauce in a sauceboat.

Yield: 4 servings
Total calories: 245

Steamed Small Artichokes with Onions

There are several kinds of artichokes. The ones used in this recipe are small with a slightly purple tinge. Cut the stems off, then with a sharp knife cut ½ inch from the tops. With a teaspoon remove the chokes. Soak the artichokes in cold water with the juice of ½ lemon so they don't turn black. You can replace the fresh artichokes with small frozen artichoke hearts, but the taste won't be the same.

> 12 small artichokes
> 1 lemon
> 1 pound small pearl onions
> 2 pounds new potatoes, washed and scrubbed
> 2 tablespoons light soy sauce
> 1-inch piece fresh ginger, grated
> salt and pepper
> chopped parsley for garnish

Prepare the artichokes as described above. Peel the onions. In a steamer, place the artichokes, potatoes, and onions. Steam, covered, for 10 minutes. Reserve the cooking water and remove the vegetables to a serving bowl.

Mix together in a bowl the soy sauce, ginger, and ¼ cup of the cooking water. Add salt and pepper and pour over the vegetables. Serve with chopped parsley sprinkled on top.

Yield: 4 servings
Total calories: 890

Steamed Okra with Sage

> 1½ pounds fresh okra
> salt and pepper
> 1 tablespoon chopped fresh sage
> 1 lemon

Wash and drain the okra and cut off the little stems. Place the okra in a steamer and steam, covered, for 4 minutes.

Remove the okra to a bowl, sprinkle with salt and pepper, mix well, then add the fresh sage and the juice of ½ the lemon or more to taste.

Serve with red snapper.

Yield: 6 servings
Total calories: 240

Steamed Okra with Earmushrooms

Earmushrooms are large clusters of whitish-gray mushrooms whose stems are attached to one another. They grow in California and are available in the spring, fresh, in specialty stores. You can replace them with large white mushrooms, which should be cut in two or in thirds.

2 pounds fresh okra
½ pound earmushrooms
1-inch piece fresh ginger, grated
1 teaspoon sesame oil
salt and pepper
juice of ½ lime
1 teaspoon black sesame seeds for garnish

Cut off the stem ends of the okra. Wash the okra and pat dry. Wash and separate the mushrooms and pat dry. Place the okra and mushrooms in a steamer, sprinkle with the grated ginger, and steam, covered, for 4 minutes. Remove to a serving bowl, add the sesame oil, salt and pepper, and the lime juice. Toss well. Sprinkle with sesame seeds and serve.

Yield: 6 servings
Total calories: 410

Baby Zucchini with Chervil

It is only in the spring or in the summer that you can find very small zucchini, which must be barely cooked. Here they are cooked with a generous amount of fresh chervil. Chervil is easy to grow on your windowsill. It can sometimes be found in specialty stores, at the first whiff of spring, but it is fragile and better if you grow your own.

> *2 pounds baby zucchini*
> *2 bunches parsley*
> *2 bunches fresh chervil*
> *coarse salt*
> *pepper*
> *¼ teaspoon nutmeg*

Wash, trim, and pat dry the zucchini. Take off a long strip of skin on each side, then cut the zucchini in two lengthwise. Wash and pat dry the parsley and chervil. Cut off the stems of both and place the stems in the boiling water under a steamer rack.

Line the steamer rack with the chervil and parsley leaves and place the zucchini on top. Steam, covered, for 5 minutes. Remove to a platter and place the parsley and chervil leaves alongside the zucchini. Sprinkle with coarse salt, pepper, and nutmeg. Serve right away.

Yield: 6 servings
Total calories: 205

Baby Zucchini with Blueberries

One evening I was invited to meet a Japanese Buddhist nun who had come here to participate in a conference. She did not speak a word of English and I, of course, not a word of Japanese. But some incredible phenomenon occurred. As I was sitting down with her, looking at her face filled with energy and laughter, I had the feeling that I understood what she was saying. Her translator told me that I should be bold in my cooking. Experiment and play with colors. I went home that evening and prepared dinner. What I made that night was mad, fun, delicious, and very much like my new Buddhist friend. Here is one of those recipes.

> 2 pounds baby zucchini, about 4 inches long
> 1 pint blueberries
> salt and pepper
> ½ cup chopped fresh basil leaves

Wash and trim the zucchini. Wash and drain the blueberries. Place the zucchini in a steamer and steam, covered, for 3 minutes, then add half the blueberries. Steam for 1 minute more.

Remove the zucchini and blueberries to a serving platter. Sprinkle with salt and pepper and the chopped basil. Add the uncooked blueberries and serve.

Yield: 6 servings
Total calories: 420

Fresh Fava Beans

> 8 large Chinese dried mushrooms
> 1 cup hot water
> 2 pounds fresh fava beans
> 2 tablespoons soy sauce
> 3 drops Oriental hot oil
> ½ tablespoon dried tarragon
> pepper
> Boston lettuce

Soak the mushrooms in the hot water for ½ hour. Shell the fava beans and set aside in a bowl of cold water. Drain the mushrooms but reserve the water; cut off the stems. Place the drained fava beans and the mushrooms in a steamer and steam, covered, for 15 minutes.

In a saucepan heat 3 tablespoons of the water from the mush-rooms and add the soy sauce and hot oil. Add the mushrooms and fava beans and heat through. Add the tarragon and pepper and serve on a bed of lettuce.

Yield: 4 servings
Total calories: 395

Fresh Lima Beans with Savory

2½ pounds fresh lima beans in the pod
salt and pepper
1 cup yogurt
2 tablespoons chopped fresh savory
juice of ½ lime

Shell the lima beans. Place the beans in a saucepan, cover with boiling water, and let stand for 2 minutes. Drain, cool, and re-move their skins. Steam the lima beans, covered, for 5 minutes. Remove to a serving bowl and sprinkle with salt and pepper.

In a small bowl beat together the yogurt, savory, and lime juice. Pour the sauce over the lima beans, toss, correct the season-ing, and serve.

Yield: 4 servings
Total calories: 690

Charcoal-Broiled Summer Corn

I spent most of my childhood in Cairo, Egypt. We lived near the Nile and in the summer my father would take me for long walks along the river's edge. About a mile from our house, there was a bridge guarded by two enormous stone lions. At the entrance of the bridge, which led to Zamaleck, another neighborhood of

Cairo, were all sorts of street merchants selling sugarcane, *foul medames* (a fava bean) in a pita bread, and charcoal-broiled corn; this was my favorite thing. The corn was tender, sweet, slightly brown. I never knew how they cooked it, but last year we went back to Egypt and I asked an old friend of the family who still lives there how it is done and she gave me these directions.

> *6 ears of corns with their husks*
> *6 tablespoons butter (1 per ear of corn)*
> *salt and pepper*
>
> *charcoal fire*

With scissors cut off any corn silk that is outside the husks. Place the corn with the husks intact in a large bowl, cover with cold water, and let them soak for 20 minutes or until the husks have absorbed some water. Prepare a charcoal fire. When the flame dies down, place the corn on the grill. You must turn the ears frequently. They will take about 15 to 20 minutes to cook. Grab them with tongs and remove the husks.

Add butter, salt, and pepper and have a feast.

Yield: 6 servings
Total calories: 1,190

Mushrooms with Herbs

Serve these mushrooms when you are roasting a chicken. Instead of using butter or any other type of fat, use a cup of the chicken cooking juices.

> *2 pounds white mushrooms*
> *2 shallots*
> *2 tablespoons chopped parsley*
> *1 tablespoon chopped chives*
> *1 tablespoon chopped fresh tarragon or ½ tablespoon dried*
> *1 cup chicken juices*
> *juice of 1 lemon*
> *salt and pepper*

Trim the mushroom stems, wash the mushrooms rapidly under cold running water, and pat dry. Peel and chop the shallots.

In a saucepan place the mushrooms, shallots, chopped herbs, chicken juices, and the lemon juice. Add salt and pepper to taste. Bring to a boil, then lower the heat, and simmer for 10 minutes. Serve with roast chicken.

Yield: 6 servings
Total calories: 340

Mushrooms with Fiddleheads and Spinach

1 pound fresh spinach
6 very large white mushrooms (3 inches in diameter)
½ pound fiddleheads
salt and pepper
3 tablespoons chopped fresh tarragon
1 tablespoon butter

Wash the spinach and remove the stems. Drain in a colander and pat dry. Wash the mushrooms, pat dry, and remove the stems (they can be used to make a mushroom soup). With a coffee spoon scoop out the inside of the mushrooms.

Wash and prepare fiddleheads as on page 63. Steam, covered, for 4 minutes in a steamer. Remove to a bowl and sprinkle with salt and pepper and the chopped tarragon. Keep warm.

In a skillet, melt the butter. Add the mushrooms, sprinkle with salt and pepper, and sauté for 3 minutes, or until they are barely cooked.

Line a serving platter with the raw spinach. Place the mushrooms on top, fill them with the fiddleheads, and serve.

Yield: 6 servings
Total calories: 275

Vegetable Terrine

I used in this recipe the vegetables that were in season the week I
first made it. You could in fact replace any of them with any
other vegetable you like, such as cauliflower, peas, eggplant, celery, etc. The principle of this kind of terrine is simply to bake the
vegetables with eggs. Serve it with a yogurt dill sauce.

½ pound carrots
½ pound leeks
½ pound white mushrooms
1 pound small zucchini
6 eggs
salt and pepper
½ cup yogurt
¼ pound low-fat farmer's cheese
1 tablespoon chopped fresh dill
3 tablespoons capers

Preheat the oven to 350°.

Scrape and slice the carrots. Trim, wash, and slice the leeks.
Trim, wash, pat dry, and slice the mushrooms. Wash and slice the
zucchini.

Steam all the vegetables except the mushrooms for 5 minutes, covered. Place all the vegetables together in a baking casserole. Beat the eggs in a bowl and add salt and pepper to taste.
Pour the eggs over the vegetables. Bake in the 350° oven in a *bain-
marie* (a pan of hot water) for 1 hour.

Meanwhile make the sauce. In a food processor beat together
the yogurt and the farmer's cheese. Add some pepper, the dill, and
the capers. Mix well and serve with the terrine.

Yield: 6 servings
Total calories: 1,050

Carrot Ring

2 eggs
3-ounce can evaporated milk
3 cups grated carrots (about 6 carrots)
salt and pepper
1 tablespoon dried oregano
2 tablespoons butter
florets of 1 bunch broccoli
½ cup blanched slivered almonds (optional)

1½-quart ring mold

Preheat the oven to 400°.

Mix together the eggs and the evaporated milk. Beat with a fork. Add the carrots to the egg mixture and add salt and pepper to taste and the oregano. Mix well.

Butter a ring mold with ½ tablespoon of the butter, spread the carrot mixture in the mold, and cover with foil. Bake in a *bain-marie* (a pan of hot water) in the 400° oven for 40 minutes.

Shortly before the carrot ring is ready, steam the broccoli, covered, for 6 minutes. Toss the florets with the remaining butter and season with salt and pepper.

Unmold the carrot ring onto a round platter, sprinkle it with the almonds, and place the broccoli florets in the center.

Yield: 6 servings
Total calories: 1,035

Cottage Cheese and Cauliflower Soufflé

1 small cauliflower
1 lemon
3 eggs
12 ounces cottage cheese (1% fat)
2 tablespoons flour
6 tablespoons yogurt
salt and pepper

1 teaspoon butter for the mold
2 tablespoons chopped chives for garnish

1-quart soufflé mold

Preheat the oven to 375°.
    Separate the cauliflower florets, removing the hard center core. Steam, covered, for 4 minutes. Set aside.
    Grate the lemon zest. Separate the eggs. In a food processor place the cottage cheese, cauliflower, egg yolks, flour, and yogurt. Run the machine until all the ingredients are puréed. Remove to a bowl. Add salt, pepper, and the lemon zest. Mix well.
    Add a pinch of salt to the egg whites and beat until stiff. Gently fold the cauliflower mixture into the egg whites. Butter a 1-quart soufflé mold. Pour the soufflé mixture gently into the mold, and bake in the 375° oven for 1 hour. Remove from the oven, sprinkle with the chopped chives, and serve immediately.

Yield: 4 servings
Total calories: 745

Chinese String-Bean Soufflés in Artichoke Bottoms

Chinese string beans are about 12 inches long. I like to use them because they are always crisp and have no strings. Steamed and left whole, they can be used as a bed for a roast chicken or for baked whole fish. Cut into 3-inch pieces and steamed, they are delicious served sprinkled with salt and chopped chives and lime juice. And they are excellent to purée and to make soufflés.

1 pound Chinese string beans
3 eggs
3 tablespoons yogurt
salt and pepper
two 14-ounce cans artichoke bottoms
1 tablespoon butter
¼ cup grated Parmesan

Preheat the oven to 425°.

Wash the string beans and cut into 3-inch pieces. Steam, covered, for 4 minutes.

Separate the eggs. In a food processor, place the string beans, egg yolks, yogurt, salt, and pepper. Run the machine until all the ingredients are puréed. Remove to a bowl. Add a pinch of salt to the egg whites and beat until stiff.

Drain the artichoke bottoms. Butter a baking dish with ½ tablespoon of butter. Place the artichokes in it, side by side. Fold the egg whites gently into the string-bean purée. Fill the artichokes with the purée, sprinkle with the Parmesan, and dot with the remaining butter. Bake in the 425° oven for 15 minutes, or until the tops are golden brown.

Serve with roast veal.

Yield: 6 servings
Total calories: 1,470

Vegetable Flan with Cherry Sauce

½ pound new baby carrots
½ celery root (or kohlrabi)
1 celery stalk
¼ pound string beans
½ pound fresh peas in their shells
5 eggs
1 soft bean curd cake
2 tablespoons chopped parsley
salt and pepper
¼ teaspoon butter for the pan (optional; see Note)

FOR THE SAUCE:

3 ripe tomatoes
1 pound fresh cherries
2 tablespoons chopped fresh tarragon
juice of ½ lime
salt and pepper

parsley for garnish

8- by 4-inch disposable aluminum-foil pound-cake pan

Scrape the carrots. Peel the celery root or the kohlrabi. Wash the celery. Cut these vegetables into small sticks about 2 inches long. Wash and trim the string beans. Shell the peas.

Fill a large saucepan with water, add ½ tablespoon salt, bring to a boil, and add all the vegetables except the peas. Bring back to a boil and cook 5 minutes. Drain the vegetables, refresh under cold running water, and pat dry with paper towels.

Preheat the oven to 375°.

In a blender, beat together the eggs, bean curd, parsley, and salt and pepper. Butter the pound-cake pan.

Spread the peas in the bottom of the pan. Then slowly pour some of the egg mixture over the peas. Cover the peas with carrots, then more egg. Continue with string beans, celery, and celery root or kohlrabi, adding egg between each layer. Bake in the 375° oven in a *bain-marie* (a pan of hot water) for 40 minutes. Remove the pan from the oven, cool, and refrigerate for 4 hours.

To make the sauce: Peel, quarter, and seed the tomatoes. Pit half the cherries. In a food processor, place the tomatoes, pitted cherries, chopped tarragon, lime juice, and salt and pepper. Run the machine until all the ingredients are puréed. Remove to a bowl and sprinkle with chopped parsley.

Unmold the flan onto a platter. Surround with the remaining cherries and with sprigs of parsley. Serve with the sauce in a sauceboat.

Yield: 6 to 8 servings
Total calories: 1,160

NOTE: Using a disposable pound-cake pan, I found that, having forgotten to butter the pan, the flan was still easy to unmold and that it was not necessary to butter the mold.

Tarte Verte

Pâte Brisée *(page 233)*
1 tablespoon butter + ½ tablespoon for the pan
1 pound fresh spinach
½ bunch watercress

1 bunch parsley
1 head escarole
1 tablespoon flour
1 cup milk
salt and pepper
¼ teaspoon nutmeg
3 eggs
3½ ounces Swiss cheese, grated
2 tablespoons chopped fresh basil leaves
1 tablespoon dried thyme

9-inch quiche pan

Preheat the oven to 375°.

Roll the pastry dough out on a floured board. Butter the quiche pan. Line the pan with the dough, prick the bottom with a fork, and bake in the 375° oven for 10 minutes. Remove from the oven and set aside.

Wash the spinach, watercress, and parsley, remove the stems, and pat all the leaves dry. Wash and pat dry the escarole. Chop all the greens with a sharp knife, not with a machine (the filling would be too watery).

In a small saucepan melt the remaining 1 tablespoon butter, add the flour, and mix well over low heat. Slowly add the milk, stirring all the time. Cook for 5 minutes. Add salt and pepper to taste, and the nutmeg.

In a small bowl, beat the eggs. Then slowly add some of the hot sauce, stirring all the time. Then add the remaining sauce. Add the egg mixture to the greens, add the cheese, basil, and thyme, and correct the seasoning.

Spread the filling in the pie shell and bake, covered with foil, in the 375° oven for 20 minutes. Remove the foil and bake for 15 minutes more.

Serve with cold chicken.

Yield: 8 servings
Total calories: 2,310

Cabbage Spring Rolls

To remain trim, but to eat something pleasing is not always easy. This past year I have also been concerned about color, texture, and mysteries. It is always fun to discover something that you did not expect in food. Take, for example, cabbage leaves. Hide in them something colorful and tasty, steam them, and serve with a light sauce. I came up with the idea of carrots, bean sprouts, fresh peas, pickled ginger, lots of lemon, and fresh basil. Steamed and served with either an herbed sauce or a very light soy sauce, the result was delicious, the taste unexpected.

1 large cabbage
6 carrots
4 slices pickled ginger (see Note)
10 fresh basil leaves
¼ pound fresh bean sprouts
1 cup shelled fresh peas
salt and pepper
juice of 1 lemon

Place the cabbage in a large saucepan, cover with water, and bring to a boil. Cook, covered, for 10 minutes. Drain, refresh under cold running water, and set aside to drain. Later, remove the core of the cabbage with a sharp knife and carefully separate the leaves. Scrape the carrots and cut them into fine julienne strips. Chop together the pickled ginger and the basil.

In a bowl, mix together the carrots, peas, bean sprouts, and ginger-and-basil mixture. Add salt and pepper and lemon juice to taste. Fill each cabbage leaf with some of the vegetable mixture and roll tightly. Place the rolls in a steamer, side by side. Steam, covered, for 5 minutes. Remove carefully to a platter and serve with a light soy sauce or Bean Curd Sauce (page 221) or Fines Herbes Sauce (page 226).

Yield: 6 servings
Total calories: 505

NOTE: Pickled ginger is sold in jars or small plastic pouches in most oriental groceries and vegetable stores. It is packed already sliced and is bright pink in color.

Cabbage Stuffed with Vegetables

This recipe is different from a regular stuffed cabbage. Here, each quarter of the cabbage is made into a miniature cabbage. Serve 1 little cabbage to each guest, with broiled chicken or Veal Burgers (page 153).

> *1 large Savoy cabbage*
> *3 carrots, chopped*
> *1 pound mushrooms, chopped*
> *3 celery stalks, chopped*
> *½ pound string beans, cut into ½-inch pieces*
> *4 tablespoons butter*
> *pepper*
> *1 tablespoon dried oregano*
> *4 onions, chopped*
> *3 garlic cloves, chopped*
> *4 tablespoons grated Gruyère*

Quarter the cabbage. In a large saucepan bring 2 quarts of water to a boil. Add the quartered cabbage and blanch for 5 minutes. Drain, cool under cold running water, and drain again. Set aside.

Bring to a boil 1 quart of water and add 1 teaspoon of salt and the carrots, mushrooms, celery, and string beans. Blanch for 5 minutes and drain immediately.

In a large skillet heat 2 tablespoons of the butter, then add all the blanched vegetables except the cabbage. Sprinkle with salt, pepper, and the oregano and cook over low heat for 5 minutes. Now add the onions and garlic and cook for another 4 minutes. Remove from the heat.

Preheat the oven to 425°.

Remove the center core of the cabbage quarters. Butter a baking dish with some of the remaining butter and spread a clean dishcloth on the table. One quarter at a time, separate the cabbage leaves. Arrange them in a circle on the cloth, the leaves overlapping each other. Place in the center ¼ of the vegetable stuffing. Close the cabbage leaves by gathering up and twisting the cloth around them. Then gently open the cloth and carefully remove the cabbage ball to the buttered baking dish. Proceed the same way with the remaining cabbage quarters.

Sprinkle 1 tablespoon of the grated Gruyère on top of each cabbage ball and add salt and pepper. Dot with the remaining butter. Bake in the 425° oven for 20 minutes or until the Gruyère is lightly browned.

Yield: 4 servings
Total calories: 1,170

Baked Stuffed Cucumbers

3 large cucumbers, unpeeled
salt
1 cup shredded carrots
4 scallions, chopped
3 garlic cloves, chopped
½ teaspoon grated fresh ginger
1 teaspoon chili powder
pepper
2 cups chicken bouillon

Preheat the oven to 425°.

Cut each cucumber into 2-inch pieces and with a small spoon remove the center seeds. Sprinkle the inside of the cucumbers with salt and set aside to drain.

Mix together the shredded carrots and the scallions, garlic, ginger, and chili powder. Add salt. Fill the centers of the cucumbers with the carrot mixture, place them in a baking dish, and sprinkle with pepper. Pour 1 cup of the chicken bouillon over the cucumbers and bake in the 425° oven for 15 minutes. Remove from the oven and arrange on a platter. Keep warm.

Add the remaining bouillon to the baking dish, scrape the sides, and, on top of the stove, reduce the liquid, over high heat, to 1 cup. Pour over the vegetables.

Serve hot with chicken or fish.

Yield: 4 servings
Total calories: 240

Endives Stuffed with Vegetables

6 endives
2 carrots
2 celery stalks
2 onions
2 shallots
salt and pepper
1 teaspoon dried thyme
1 tablespoon butter
½ cup chicken bouillon

Preheat the oven to 425°.

Wash the endives. Cut them in two lengthwise and remove some of the center leaves so as to have room for the stuffing. Reserve the center leaves. Place the endive halves in an ovenproof dish.

Cut the carrots into julienne strips. Trim the celery and cut it into julienne strips. Peel and chop the onion and shallots. Chop the center leaves of endives.

Mix all the vegetables together. Sprinkle with salt and pepper and the thyme. Heat the butter in a skillet, add the vegetables, and cook over low heat for 5 minutes. Then fill the endives with the vegetable mixture. Pour the chicken bouillon over them and bake in the 425° oven for 30 minutes, basting from time to time.
Serve with chicken or lamb.

Yield: 6 servings
Total calories: 420

Kohlrabi Stuffed with Spinach

4 kohlrabi
1 pound fresh spinach
1 soft cake bean curd
1 garlic clove
salt and pepper
½ tablespoon olive oil
3 radishes, washed and sliced, for garnish

Peel the kohlrabi and cut them in two. Cut off a very thin slice on the round side of each half so they can stand easily. Steam the kohlrabi in a steamer, covered, for 6 to 8 minutes until tender. Cool. With a melon-ball cutter remove some of the center of each piece to make wells 2 inches across. Set the kohlrabi balls aside.

Trim and wash the spinach and pat dry. Steam, covered, for 3 minutes. Refresh under cold running water, then squeeze with your hands to remove all the water. In a food processor, place the spinach, bean curd, and garlic and run the machine until all the ingredients are puréed. Correct the seasoning with salt and pepper.

Brush the kohlrabi with olive oil and sprinkle with salt and pepper. Fill each well with some of the spinach. Place the stuffed kohlrabi and the reserved kohlrabi balls in the steamer and steam, covered, to reheat for 2 minutes before serving. To serve, place the kohlrabi on a platter and garnish with the sliced radishes and the small kohlrabi balls.

Yield: 8 servings
Total calories: 600

Kohlrabi Stuffed with Carrot Purée

6 kohlrabi, preferably small ones
salt and pepper
1 cup carrot purée (Orange Purée, page 180)
2 tablespoons chopped chives (instead of tarragon in purée
  recipe)
3 shallots, very finely chopped

Peel the kohlrabi and with a spoon make a hole in the center of each one about the size of a 50-cent piece and about 1 inch deep. Steam the kohlrabi, covered, for 3 minutes or until tender. (Spring kohlrabi are very tender, winter ones may take 6 to 8 minutes.) Sprinkle with salt and pepper.

To the carrot purée, add the chives and the chopped shallots. Fill the kohlrabi with the purée, mounding it slightly. Put back in the steamer for 2 minutes, covered, to reheat before serving.

Serve with roast chicken, veal, or fish.

Yield: 6 servings
Total calories: 540

Asparagus Salad with Beets

In the spring, when the asparagus are very thin, is the time to make this salad.

16-ounce can baby beets
1 pound thin new asparagus
½ cup Soy Vinegar Dressing (page 220)
2 tablespoons chopped parsley for garnish

Drain the beets and put in a salad bowl. Cut 2 inches off the bottom of the asparagus stalks, wash the asparagus under cold running water, and cut into 1-inch pieces. Steam, covered, for 3 minutes, until barely tender. Add the asparagus to the beets, pour the dressing over them, toss gently, and refrigerate until ready to serve. Sprinkle the salad with chopped parsley just before serving.

Yield: 4 servings
Total calories: 240

Apple and Beet Salad

12-ounce can whole beets
3 firm McIntosh apples
juice of ½ lemon
1 cup yogurt
1 teaspoon grated lemon rind
salt and pepper

Drain the beets and slice. Peel and core the apples and chop coarsely. Put in a bowl with the lemon juice. In a bowl, mix together the yogurt and lemon rind and add salt and pepper to taste.

In a serving bowl, mix together the apples and sliced beets, pour the yogurt over them, toss, and serve.

Yield: 4 servings
Total calories: 430

Red Cabbage Salad

1 large red cabbage
2 tablespoons sesame oil
2 tablespoons light soy sauce
1 tablespoon rice vinegar
salt and pepper
1 tablespoon black sesame seeds

Remove the central core and the tough outer leaves of the cabbage. Quarter the cabbage, then slice it very thin. In a large frying pan, heat the oil, add the cabbage, and sauté for 2 minutes. Then add the soy sauce, vinegar, and salt and pepper to taste. Mix well and cook for another 3 minutes. Remove to a salad bowl, sprinkle with the sesame seeds, and refrigerate.

Serve cold with chicken or fish.

Yield: 6 servings
Total calories: 535

Red and Green Cabbage Salad with Apples

This dish should be made in a glass salad bowl so that the different colors of the pattern can be seen.

1 small red cabbage
1 small green cabbage
4 Granny Smith apples
½ cup Yogurt Sauce (page 221)
2 teaspoons black sesame seeds

Remove the outer leaves and the central core of both cabbages. Cut the cabbages into chunks and shred them with the slicing blade of a food processor. Peel and core the apples and cut them into julienne strips.

Line a glass salad bowl first with the green cabbage, then add the red cabbage, then the apples. Pour the dressing over the salad, sprinkle the top with the black sesame seeds, and bring to the table. Toss at the table.

Yield: 6 servings
Total calories: 855

Fennel Salad with Apples and Cranberries

1 cup fresh cranberries
¼ cup sugar
¼ cup water
2 fennel bulbs
2 Granny Smith apples
juice of 1 lemon
1 teaspoon mustard
2 shallots, chopped
½ cup yogurt
salt and pepper
2 ounces blue cheese, crumbled

Wash the cranberries and cook them with the sugar and ¼ cup water until the cranberries pop. Set aside to cool.

Remove the outside layer of the fennel bulbs; they are sometimes bitter. Wash, pat dry, and cut the fennel into julienne strips with a sharp knife. Peel and core the Granny Smith apples. Slice them thin and place in a salad bowl with ½ the lemon juice. Add the fennel and toss.

In a small bowl mix together the mustard, shallots, yogurt, the remaining lemon juice, and salt and pepper to taste. Mix well and add to the fennel and apples. Toss. Sprinkle with the blue cheese and place the cranberries in the center. Serve at room temperature, with cold chicken or turkey.

Yield: 6 servings
Total calories: 905

Sugar Snap Peas and Radish Salad

1 pound sugar snap peas
1 bunch radishes
3 tablespoons yogurt
1 tablespoon lemon juice
salt and pepper
2 tablespoons chopped fresh basil leaves

Snap the ends off the peas, wash them, and steam, covered, for 3 minutes. Refresh immediately under cold running water and drain. Cut off the stems and tips of the radishes, wash very carefully, pat dry, and slice thin. Place the sugar snaps in a serving bowl with the radishes.

In a small bowl mix together the yogurt, lemon juice, salt and pepper, and fresh basil. Mix well, add to the salad, toss well, and serve. (The salad should not be refrigerated but served at room temperature.)

Yield: 4 servings
Total calories: 185

Chinese White Radish Salad

Chinese white radish is about 4 to 6 inches long, and 2 to 3 inches in diameter. Cut into a julienne or grated, served with fish or in soup, it is a very tasty vegetable. Here it is served with apples in a light soy sauce with hot peppers. Serve this salad with baked fish.

> 1 large Chinese white radish
> 2 Granny Smith apples
> 3 scallions, sliced thin
> 3 tablespoons light soy sauce
> 1 tablespoon oil
> 1 teaspoon toasted white sesame seeds (see Note page 220)
> ½ teaspoon hot crushed red peppers
> salt and pepper

Peel the radish and cut it into julienne strips. Peel and core the apples and slice thin. Make the dressing by combining the remaining ingredients. Put the radish with the apples in a bowl, pour the dressing over them, toss, and serve.

Yield: 4 servings
Total calories: 475

Bean Sprout Salad with Arugola

Arugola has a sharp taste but mixed with bean sprouts, it is more pleasant to the palate and very refreshing.

1 pound fresh bean sprouts
2 bunches arugola
3 tablespoons light soy sauce
juice of ½ lemon
1 garlic clove, crushed
2 scallions, chopped fine
1 tablespoon sesame seeds
salt and pepper

Wash the arugola, pat dry, and cut off the stems. Toss the arugola and bean sprouts together in a bowl. In another bowl, mix together the soy sauce, lemon juice, garlic, scallions, and sesame seeds. Add salt and pepper to taste and pour over the salad. Toss and serve.

Yield: 6 servings
Total calories: 290

Chayote or "Green Pear" Salad

Chayote is a West Indian and Caribbean vegetable. It looks like a pale green pear, but it belongs to the family of squash. It can be baked, boiled, steamed, it has a cool refreshing taste, and served with Soy Vinegar Dressing it is delicious.

3 chayotes
½ cup Soy Vinegar Dressing (page 220)
2 tablespoons chopped parsley

Wash, peel, and pit the chayotes and cut them into slices about ½ inch thick. Place the slices in a steamer and steam, covered, for 6 to 8 minutes. Remove the chayotes to a serving platter and pour the dressing over them while they are still hot. Sprinkle with the parsley and serve at room temperature.

Yield: 4 servings
Total calories: 205

Kohlrabi Salad with Bibb Lettuce

Kohlrabi is a strange-looking vegetable. It is a plump ball with, coming up from the base, long strings that look like the arms of R2D2 of *Star Wars*. Its delicate flavor makes it excellent served raw, as in this salad.

3 kohlrabi
4 small heads Bibb lettuce
1 tablespoon chopped parsley
½ cup Soy Vinegar Dressing (page 220)

Peel the kohlrabi and cut into julienne strips either with a sharp knife or with the julienne blade of a food processor. Set aside. Wash and pat dry the Bibb lettuce and cut the heads in two lengthwise.

On a round platter place first the Bibb lettuce in a circle. In the center pile the julienne of kohlrabi. Sprinkle with chopped parsley and pour the soy dressing over the salad. Serve with cold meats.

Yield: 4 servings
Total calories: 495

Hot New Potato Salad with Red Lumpfish Caviar

When our children were small we used to summer in East Hampton. The house was next to an enormous potato field. In late August I would send my daughters out with a basket to pick the smallest potatoes. They used to tiptoe to the field when no one was looking and, with a large serving spoon, dig for the small potatoes. (Local people call them "gleanings." The farmer would look the other way, but he would later lecture me on the goodness of the large potatoes in the market.) We would wash and scrub them only, not peel them, and make a delicious hot potato salad. It can be garnished with any leftovers you have in the refrigerator—cold chicken, beef, fish, seafood, etc. Here I serve it with red lumpfish caviar. As for your potatoes, use white new potatoes as small as you can find them in the market or use the smallest red ones.

2 pounds small potatoes
juice of 1 lemon
2 tablespoons oil

1 teaspoon cumin
1 teaspoon paprika
1 garlic clove, chopped
salt and pepper
3 scallions, sliced thin
2 tablespoons chopped parsley
2-ounce jar red lumpfish caviar

Wash and scrub the potatoes. Steam them, covered, for 15 minutes or until they feel tender when pricked with a fork. Remove to a large bowl. Cut the larger ones in two.

Make the dressing in a bowl with the lemon and oil, cumin, paprika, garlic, and salt and pepper. Pour it over the hot potatoes and add the scallions and parsley. Toss well, then sprinkle with the red lumpfish caviar, and serve.

Yield: 6 servings
Total calories: 905

Lentil Salad

Lentils are the oldest bean in the world and one of the best. Served cold with scallions and garlic, they are a marvelous addition to any cold meat dish.

1 pound lentils, rinsed
1 onion stuck with 2 cloves
½ cup yogurt
juice of ½ lemon
salt and pepper
2 garlic cloves, chopped
4 scallions, sliced

Put the lentils in a large saucepan, cover with water, add the onion stuck with 2 cloves, and bring to a boil. Simmer until the lentils are just cooked, or about 25 minutes. Drain.

In a salad bowl mix together the yogurt, lemon juice, and salt and pepper. Add the lentils, chopped garlic, and scallions. Toss well, correct seasoning, and refrigerate until ready to serve.

Yield: 6 servings
Total calories: 1,720

Tabouli Salad

Tabouli is cracked wheat or bulgur. It is sold in supermarkets. The secret of a good *tabouli* salad is the freshness of the parsley. My Egyptian grandmother used to say: 1 cup of *tabouli* to 1 cup of fresh parsley. *Tabouli* is excellent served with broiled fish or broiled chicken.

> *1 cup bulgur or cracked wheat*
> *½ cup lemon juice*
> *3 tablespoons olive oil*
> *1 cup chopped parsley*
> *¼ cup chopped fresh mint*
> *¼ cup chopped scallions*
> *salt and pepper*
> *4 ripe tomatoes, peeled, seeded, and chopped*

In a bowl place the bulgur, cover with cold water, mix with a wooden spoon, and let stand for 30 minutes. When you chop the herbs, be sure to pat them very dry first.

In another bowl mix together the lemon juice and olive oil. Add the herbs and scallions and season to taste with salt and pepper.

Drain the water, if there is any left, from the bulgur. Add the tomatoes and the dressing to the bulgur, mix well, and correct seasoning.

Yield: 4 servings
Total calories: 855

DRESSINGS & SAUCES

Here are a few sauces and dressings, most of which you can make ahead and store in the refrigerator. They are referred to in various parts of this book.

Soy Vinegar Dressing for Salad

6 tablespoons light soy sauce
2 tablespoons rice vinegar
2 scallions, sliced thin
1 garlic clove, chopped fine
1 teaspoon sesame seeds, crushed (see Note)
pepper

Mix all the ingredients together and store in a jar with a tight lid. You need 2½ tablespoons for a salad to serve 4. This dressing will keep in the refrigerator for a week.

Yield: about ½ cup or 4 servings
Total calories: 90

NOTE: Sesame seeds are available in supermarkets and in health-food stores. There are white and black sesame seeds. The black sesame seeds do not need to be toasted. White sesame seeds should be toasted before they are used: Heat a skillet, add 1 teaspoon sesame seeds, and heat them for 3 minutes, shaking the pan continuously. Let the seeds cool, then crush in a mortar with a pestle, and add to your dressing.

Soy Sauce with Japanese Horseradish

1 teaspoon Japanese horseradish (wasabi)
¼ cup water
¼ cup light soy sauce

In a bowl mix together well the *wasabi* and 1 tablespoon water, then add the soy sauce and the ¼ cup of water. This sauce can be stored in a jar and refrigerated for a week.

Yield: about ½ cup
Total calories: 50

NOTE: You usually need about 2 tablespoons of this sauce to season vegetables, chicken, or fish.

Yogurt Sauce

½ cup low-fat yogurt
juice of ½ lemon
¼ teaspoon cumin
1 garlic clove, chopped very fine
salt and pepper

In a bowl mix together all the ingredients. Correct the seasoning, adding more pepper if necessary.

Yield: about ½ cup
Total calories: 80

Bean Curd Sauce

This sauce is a delicious substitute for the mayonnaise-based sauces that you would normally serve with cold fish or chicken dishes and with terrines.

1 bunch fresh spinach or 2 bunches watercress
1 soft bean curd cake
1 garlic clove, sliced
2 scallions, sliced

1 teaspoon sesame oil
¼ cup water (more if the sauce has to be thin, for
artichokes, for example)
salt and pepper

Wash and pat dry the spinach and remove all the stems. In a food processor, place the bean curd, spinach, garlic, scallions, and sesame oil. Run the machine until all the ingredients are puréed. Then while the machine is still running, add the water. Remove to a bowl and correct the seasoning with salt and pepper.

Yield: 2 cups
Total calories: 220

Vegetable Sauce, Hot or Cold

When you are on a diet, sauces become something of a sin. No sauces, say the diet books! But if you want to make a dish more interesting and crave a rich sauce, here is one that is delicious, hot or cold, a sauce that is thick and has only one sinful ingredient, a tablespoon of olive oil. Serve it with anything and everything. Change it with spices to suit your mood or add any fresh herbs you may have grown or can buy.

2 shallots
2 medium-size carrots
1 celery stalk
1 pound ripe tomatoes
1 tablespoon olive oil
salt and pepper
1 sprig fresh thyme
1 cup finely chopped celery leaves
¼ cup water or tomato juice
2 tablespoons very good wine vinegar

Peel and chop the shallots. Scrape the carrots and chop fine. Wash the celery stalk and chop fine. Wash, quarter, and seed the tomatoes. Chop and set aside.

In a heavy saucepan, heat the oil and add the shallots, carrots, and celery. Mix well, add salt and pepper to taste, and cover with the thyme and celery leaves. Reduce the heat, cover, and simmer for 10 minutes. Remove the thyme and then add the tomatoes and ¼ cup water or tomato juice. Mix well, cover, and simmer for 30 minutes.

Purée the sauce in a food processor or blender. Return it to the saucepan, heat, and correct the seasoning. Add the vinegar, mix well, and serve.

If the sauce is to be served cold, refrigerate, covered, until ready to use. It will keep for at least a week.

Yield: 1½ cups
Total calories: 335

Curry Sauce

This is a spicy sauce to use with terrines and meat pâtés or any cold meat.

2 large ripe tomatoes
2 or 3 leaves (or to taste) Chinese parsley (coriander)
1 pound cottage cheese (1% fat)
1½ teaspoons curry powder
salt and pepper

Dip the tomatoes in boiling water and refresh immediately under cold running water. Drain, peel, quarter, and seed. Place the tomatoes in a food processor with the parsley and cottage cheese and run the machine until all the ingredients are puréed. Remove to a bowl and add the curry and salt and pepper to taste. Mix well and refrigerate the sauce until ready to use. It will keep in a tightly covered jar for at least a week.

Yield: 2 cups
Total calories: 485

Parsley Sauce

1 large bunch parsley, stems removed
4 slices avocado, 1 inch thick
juice of ½ lime
½ teaspoon cumin
salt and pepper
½ cup hot water

Wash the parsley and dry thoroughly in paper towels. Place all the ingredients in a food processor and run the machine until they are well puréed. Correct the seasoning, pour into a bowl, and refrigerate until ready to use. This sauce will keep a week in a tightly covered jar.

Yield: 1½ cups
Total calories: 210

Stewed Tomatoes

16-ounce can stewed whole tomatoes
½ tablespoon olive oil
1 garlic clove, chopped
¼ cup chopped fresh basil leaves
juice of ½ lime
salt and pepper

Drain the tomatoes. In a saucepan heat the olive oil, add the chopped garlic, and sauté for 2 minutes over medium heat. (The garlic must not brown.) Add the tomatoes, basil, lime juice, and salt and pepper. Heat gently and mix carefully with a wooden spoon; the tomatoes are quite fragile and break easily. They do not have to cook; just heat through. Serve immediately.

Yield: 4 servings
Total calories: 200

Fresh Tomato Sauce

To make this sauce a real triumph, you need ripe summer tomatoes. If you do it in the winter with hothouse tomatoes, add ½ teaspoon of tomato paste to give it more color.

1 large bunch parsley, stems removed
2 garlic cloves
2 shallots
6 Greek black olives (optional)
3 large tomatoes
¼ cup tomato juice
salt and pepper

Wash the parsley and dry thoroughly in paper towels. Peel the garlic and shallots. Pit the black olives. Dip the tomatoes in boiling water, refresh under cold running water, drain, and peel. Quarter the tomatoes and remove all the seeds.

In a food processor, chop together the parsley, garlic, shallots, and olives. Then add the tomatoes. Chop coarsely; do not purée. Transfer the mixture to a saucepan and add the tomato juice and salt and pepper. Mix well and heat but *do not boil.*

Serve with chicken, fish, or vegetables.

Yield: 2 cups
Total calories: 185

Sorrel Sauce for Vegetables

One day I bought sorrel in the supermarket (they call it sour grass), intending to serve it as a vegetable to my guests, one of whom was a vegetarian. That night I had cooked yellow squash, fava beans with a lemon dressing, and I would also serve the sorrel. I cooked the sorrel, left it on the stove, and forgot about it. When I came back to the kitchen, the bottom of the pan was almost scorched and on top was a thick green sauce. I saved some and served it on the squash. Everyone thought it was delicious and a new sauce was born.

2 pounds sorrel
1 egg
½ cup milk
salt and pepper
pinch of nutmeg
1 tablespoon sugar, or sparingly to taste

Wash and trim the sorrel and pat dry. Plunge the sorrel into ½ quart of boiling salted water and cook for 3 minutes. Drain and squeeze out the water.

Place the sorrel, egg, milk, salt and pepper, and nutmeg in a food processor. Run the machine until all the sorrel is puréed. Remove the sorrel to a saucepan and cook over high heat until it dries up and thickens. Add sugar to taste, just to moderate the tartness of the sorrel. Serve with steamed yellow squash or other vegetables.

Yield: 2 cups
Total calories: 385

Fines Herbes Sauce

This is a very versatile sauce for broiled meat such as steak or chicken. It can be stored in the refrigerator for about 1 week.

½ cup dry red wine
4 shallots, chopped
1½ tablespoons each chopped fresh tarragon, chervil, and
*   chives (or ½ tablespoon each if dried)*
1½ cups chicken broth
juice of ½ lemon
salt and pepper

Place all the ingredients in a saucepan, slowly bring to a boil, reduce the heat, and simmer for 10 minutes. Correct the seasoning. Strain through a fine sieve and store in the refrigerator until needed.

Yield: 2 cups
Total calories: 125

DESSERTS

Chinese Pears with Cranberries

Chinese pears are round, like apples, pale yellow, and their flesh is white and very crisp. It is a delicious fruit.

>   1 package cranberries
>   ½ cup sugar
>   1 cup water
>   6 Chinese pears
>   12 fresh mint leaves for garnish

Wash the cranberries. In a saucepan place the cranberries, sugar, and water and cook over medium heat until all the berries have popped. Put the cranberries in a 9-inch glass pie pan or shallow serving bowl and refrigerate.

Peel the pears. With a teaspoon scoop out the center cores from the bottoms of the pears. Place the pears in the cranberries in a circle, garnish with mint leaves, and serve.

Yield: 6 servings
Total calories: 1,105

Cranberries with Clementines

Clementines are very small tangerines with no seeds. In France, clementines bring to mind an old-fashioned pink and white lady with ribbons and flowers, in love with some long-gone young man. Do you remember those old-fashioned postcards with hearts and kisses? They were for Clementine. On the postcards the lady had a very small waist. This recipe will help you keep yours.

>   6 clementines
>   ½ package fresh cranberries
>   ½ cup sugar
>   ½ cup orange juice
>   ¼ cup water
>   parsley for garnish

Peel the clementines, reserving the rinds. Cut each clementine in two crosswise. Chop the rind fine. Wash and drain the cranberries.

In a saucepan place the cranberries, sugar, orange juice, water, and the chopped rind. Cook over medium heat until the cranberries pop. Pour the cranberries into a 9-inch glass pie dish or shallow serving bowl. Roll the clementines in the cranberries, then arrange them, cut side down, in the dish. Garnish with small parsley sprigs. Refrigerate until ready to serve.

Yield: 6 servings
Total calories: 740

Pomegranate and Melon

Pomegranate is a beautiful red fruit whose bitter taste is very refreshing in the summer. The name comes from the French, meaning "seedy apple." Beneath its red skin you will find a bright ruby-like interior of hundreds of little seeds. These seeds are tender and juicy with a tart, spicy taste. The seeds are easily dislodged by first cracking the fruit in half. Rub your fingers with lemon, as emptying the fruit may stain your fingers.

2 large cantaloupes
1 large pomegranate
4 tablespoons sugar
4 fresh mint leaves for garnish

Cut each cantaloupe in half and remove the seeds. Over a bowl, in order to catch the juice, cut the pomegranate in two. Scoop the seeds and all the juice into the bowl. Sprinkle them with the sugar, and refrigerate until ready to serve. Just before serving, fill the melon cavities with the pomegranate seeds and juice and garnish with the mint leaves.

Yield: 4 servings
Total calories: 615

Fresh Red Currants

Fresh currants are now appearing in New York markets, and I hope elsewhere too. They are tiny red berries that grow in clusters. Even when ripe, they have a slightly sour taste, but in the spring and the early part of summer, I do not know of a more refreshing or delightful dessert.

> 2 pints red currants
> 2 tablespoons sugar
> 1 pint raspberries
> 6 fresh mint leaves for garnish

Carefully remove the currants from their tiny stems. Place the berries in a colander and quickly rinse them under cold running water. Drain and put in a serving bowl. Sprinkle the sugar on top, toss well, then refrigerate for at least 1 hour.

Meanwhile, carefully wash the raspberries and purée in a food processor. Just before serving, pour the raspberry purée over the currants, toss, and serve garnished with the mint leaves.

Yield: 6 servings
Total calories: 595

Poached Pears in Wine with Cassis

> 6 Anjou pears
> ¼ cup cassis preserves (see Note)
> 2 cups red wine
> 1 tablespoon soy sauce
> ¼ cup sugar
> 6 fresh mint leaves for garnish

Peel the pears, leaving them whole and the stems on. With a teaspoon, core the pears from the bottom end.

Over a bowl drain the cassis preserves in a small strainer. Set aside the cassis berries. In a large saucepan, combine the wine, soy sauce, sugar, and the cassis liquid. Bring to a boil, add the pears, and simmer for 15 minutes, or until the pears feel tender when pierced with a fork.

Remove the pears to a serving bowl. When they are cool, lift them up gently and fill the cavities with the cassis berries. Boil down the cooking juice to about 1½ cups, pour it over the pears, and refrigerate until ready to serve. Serve garnished with the mint leaves.

Yield: 6 servings
Total calories: 1,415

NOTE: Cassis preserves are black currants preserved in a light syrup. They are imported from France and are sold in specialty stores.

Melon aux Fruits de Saison

Summer is the most fun for dessert for then you can play with all kinds of fruit. Here a small melon, 1 per person, is filled with whatever fruit is available in the market that day.

4 small cantaloupes
2 kiwis
½ pound cherries
4 plums
4 apricots
1 mango
12 perfect strawberries
½ pint red currants + 1 teaspoon sugar (optional)
1 lime
fresh mint leaves or parsley for garnish

Cut off the tops of the cantaloupes about ⅓ of the way down. With a spoon remove all the seeds. Cut the edges of the melons in zigzag "teeth" all around. With a melon-ball cutter remove as much melon meat as possible. Put the melon balls in a bowl. Scrape out the rest of the melon meat and discard.

Peel and slice the kiwis. Add to the bowl with the melon. Wash the cherries, remove the stems, and add to the bowl. Wash the plums, cut in two, remove the pits, and add to the bowl. Do the same for the apricots. Peel the mango and cut into bite-size pieces. Add to the bowl and mix the fruits gently. Wash and drain the strawberries and set aside. Remove the red currants from their stems to a bowl, wash and drain, then sprinkle with the sugar.

Fill each melon with some of the fruit from the bowl. Finish with 3 strawberries on top, then add some red currants. Squeeze some lime juice over the fruit and refrigerate until ready to serve.

Garnish with mint leaves or small parsley sprigs.

Yield: 4 servings
Total calories: 1,340

Strawberry Quiche

Pâte Brisée *(page 233)*
½ tablespoon butter for the pan
6 egg yolks
½ cup sugar
8 ounces cottage cheese
2 pints strawberries

9-inch quiche pan

Preheat the oven to 400°.

Roll the pastry dough out on a floured board. Butter the quiche pan, line the pan with the dough, and prick the bottom with a fork. Bake in the 400° oven for 15 minutes. Remove from the oven and let cool. Lower the oven heat to 375°.

In a bowl, beat together the egg yolks and the sugar, add the cottage cheese, and beat again. Wash and hull the strawberries. Fill the crust with the berries and pour the egg-and-cheese mixture over them. Bake the quiche in the 375° oven for 35 minutes.

Serve at room temperature.

Yield: 8 servings
Total calories: 3,350

Cheese Pie with Strawberries

FOR THE PÂTE BRISÉE:

1¾ cups unsifted flour
1 stick (¼ pound) butter, chilled and cut in pieces + ½
        tablespoon for the pan
¼ teaspoon salt
1 egg
1 tablespoon oil
¼ cup ice water

9-inch pie pan

FOR THE FILLING:

2 egg whites
3 envelopes unflavored gelatin
1 tablespoon cold water
juice of 2 lemons
1 pound low-fat farmer's cheese
1 cup yogurt
¼ cup rum
⅔ cup sugar
2 pints strawberries
¼ cup raspberry jelly

Make the pastry dough. In a food processor place the flour, butter, and salt. Run the machine until the dough has the consistency of coarse meal. In a small pitcher combine the egg, oil, and ice water. With the machine running, slowly add the egg mixture. Run the machine until the dough forms a ball. Remove and refrigerate, covered, for 1 hour.

Preheat the oven to 400°.

Roll out the dough on a floured board. Butter the pie pan, line it with the dough, and prick with a fork. Bake in the 400° oven for 15 minutes or until golden brown. Remove from the oven and let cool.

Make the filling. Beat the egg whites until stiff. In a bowl soak the gelatin in 1 tablespoon of cold water and add the lemon juice. Place the bowl in a saucepan of simmering water and stir until the gelatin is completely dissolved.

Beat together the cheese and the yogurt. Add the gelatin and rum and mix well. Add the sugar and mix well. Then gently fold in the egg whites. Fill the piecrust with the cheese mixture and refrigerate until ready to serve (about 1½ hours).

Hull the strawberries. Just before serving, garnish the pie with the berries. In a small saucepan melt the raspberry jelly, cool, and brush the strawberries with it.

Yield: 6 to 8 servings
Total calories: 4,060

Swiss Chard Pie

This is an old Provençal recipe that I first had when I was a young girl and we were spending the summer in Aix-en-Provence. In the small *pension* where we were staying, we had Swiss chard nearly every other day. I hated it and refused to eat it, offending Madame Jeannette, the owner of the *pension*. One day she served a wonderful pie, but I was passed by. When I asked why, she said with a very mischievous smile: *"Mais, Mademoiselle Colette, vous n'aimez pas les blettes."* From that day on I always ate her vegetables, fearing that when there was a wonderful dessert such as that one, I would again be forgotten.

Pâte Brisée *(page 233)*
1 pound Swiss chard
4 teaspoons flour
4 egg yolks
pinch of salt
½ cup sugar
½ cup milk
½ teaspoon vanilla extract
½ tablespoon butter for the pan
juice of ½ lemon
fresh strawberries or 1 tablespoon confectioners' sugar for
        garnish

9-inch pie pan

Refrigerate the pie dough while preparing the filling.

Cut off the stems of the Swiss chard and discard. Wash the chard, place it in a large saucepan, cover with cold water, bring to a boil, and remove from the heat. Drain and refresh the chard under cold running water, then squeeze it with your hands to remove all the water. Chop coarsely with a sharp knife and place in a fine sieve over a bowl to drain.

Preheat the oven to 400°.

In a food processor, place the flour, egg yolks, and a pinch of salt. Run the machine until the ingredients are well mixed, then add the sugar, mix again. Heat the milk. Then slowly, with the machine running, add the milk to the egg mixture. Pour into a bowl and stir in the vanilla.

On a floured board, roll out the dough. Butter the pie pan and line it with the dough. Prick the bottom and bake in the 400° oven for 15 minutes. Remove from the oven and let cool.

Add the chopped chard to the egg mixture, add the lemon juice, and mix well. Pour the filling into the pie pan and bake in the 400° oven for 35 minutes. Serve at room temperature with a *coulis* (purée) of strawberries or just with a tablespoon of confectioners' sugar sprinkled on top.

Yield: 6 to 8 servings
Total calories: 2,160

Strawberry Soup

This dessert is not really a strawberry soup but does have to be served in bowls and eaten with a spoon. The recipe was given to me by an old lady, Mrs. Cook, who has a strawberry farm. Every spring we go and pick our own berries there. One summer, having picked too much, I didn't quite know what to do with so many strawberries. When Mrs. Cook gave me her recipe, she told us that she had it at her wedding forty-five years before and that she still had a wonderful memory of that day!

1 bottle dry white wine
12 fresh mint leaves
2 to 3 pounds fresh strawberries
¼ cup wine vinegar
⅝ cup sugar

Pour the wine into a large glass bowl and add 5 or 6 mint leaves. Cover the wine and refrigerate for 3 hours.

Meanwhile, hull the strawberries and wash them in water to which you have added the vinegar. Drain. Slice half the strawberries, combine all the berries in a bowl, sprinkle them with the sugar, and toss well. One hour before serving, remove the mint leaves from the wine and add the strawberries. Cover and set aside for 1 hour; do not refrigerate, or the strawberries will wilt. Just before serving, chop the remaining mint and sprinkle the "soup" with it.

Yield: 8 servings
Total calories: 1,020

Cantaloupe Cake

FOR THE CRUST:

5 ounces graham crackers
3 tablespoons melted butter
¼ cup sugar
flour
½ tablespoon butter for the pan

FOR THE FILLING:

1 small ripe cantaloupe
8 ounces cottage cheese (1% fat)
½ cup yogurt
2 egg yolks
⅔ cup sugar
1 lemon
1 tablespoon brandy

3 envelopes unflavored gelatin
3 tablespoons water
6 fresh mint leaves for garnish

9-inch quiche pan

Make the crust. In a food processor place the graham crackers and run the machine until they are reduced to a fine meal, then slowly add the melted butter and the sugar. Remove the mixture to a floured board, flatten it with a rolling pin, then with it, piece by piece, line the buttered quiche pan. Refrigerate.

Cut the melon in two, remove the seeds, and scoop out the meat in pieces. In a food processor place the melon, cheese, yogurt, egg yolks, and sugar. Run the machine until all the ingredients are puréed. Add the juice of ½ the lemon and the brandy. Mix.

In a small bowl soak the gelatin in 3 tablespoons water. Place the bowl in a saucepan of simmering water and stir the gelatin until it is totally dissolved. Add to the melon mixture and mix well. Pour the mixture into the quiche crust and refrigerate for at least 1 hour.

Serve garnished with slices of the remaining ½ lemon and mint leaves.

Yield: 6 servings
Total calories: 2,295

Passion Fruit Sherbet

Passion fruit is a tropical fruit with a smooth, dark brown skin, which wrinkles like an old man's face when the fruit is really ripe. Inside are tiny little seeds whose surrounding flesh, a pale gelatinous yellow substance, has a marvelous exotic taste. There are very few things one can do with passion fruit except eat them fresh with a teaspoon, scooping up the seeds with their juice, or make ice cream or sherbet. You can make the sherbet just before dinner if you own one of those new ice cream makers that will churn ice cream or sherbet in no time. If you don't—and I don't—you can make the sherbet in the morning for that evening's dinner.

3 cups water
½ cup + 2 tablespoons sugar
12 passion fruit
2 egg whites
pinch of salt
1 tablespoon confectioners' sugar
4 fresh mint leaves for garnish

Pour the water and the sugar into a saucepan and heat until all the sugar has dissolved. Cool the syrup. Cut the passion fruit in two and scoop out all the seeds into a bowl. Then pour the seeds into a fine sieve and with the back of a wooden spoon press over a bowl to extract all the juice. Add the juice to the syrup. Add a pinch of salt, mix well, pour the mixture into ice cube trays, and place in the freezer until it is all frozen to a mush, but not hard.

Meanwhile, beat the egg whites until nearly stiff, then add the confectioners' sugar and beat until stiff. Remove the passion ice from the freezer and add the egg whites to it. Mix well and return the sherbet to the freezer compartment. Remove from the freezer an hour later and beat with an electric beater. Place back in the freezer. Do this 3 times.

Five minutes before serving, remove the sherbet to the refrigerator section to soften. Use an ice cream scooper and serve 2 scoops to each guest. Garnish with mint leaves.

If you have an ice cream maker, follow the manufacturer's directions for freezing sherbets.

Yield: 4 servings
Total calories: 805

Crêpes Stuffed with Fresh Fruits

3 eggs
3 tablespoons sugar
¾ cup water
1 cup milk
grated rind of 1 orange
2 tablespoons butter
2 cups diced fruit (peaches, apricots, mangoes, plums, etc.)

Beat together the eggs and the sugar and gradually add the water. Then slowly add the milk, stirring until you have a smooth batter. Add the orange rind and mix well.

In a crêpe pan heat ½ tablespoon of the butter. When it is hot add just enough batter to cover the bottom of the pan. Cook over medium heat until bubbles form on the surface, then, with a spatula, turn the crêpe over and cook for another 2 minutes. Remove to a heated platter and continue making crêpes until all the batter has been used, adding butter sparingly to the pan as needed.

Fill the hot crêpes with the diced fruit and serve right away.

Yield: 12 crêpes, 6 servings
Total calories: 2,135

Honey Cake

5 eggs, separated
2 tablespoons sugar
⅓ cup + 1 tablespoon flour
4 ounces (⅓ cup) honey
½ cup chopped hazelnuts
2 tablespoons ricotta cheese
½ tablespoon butter for the pan

9-inch quiche pan

Preheat the oven to 375°.

In a food processor place the egg yolks, sugar, flour, and honey. Run the machine until the mixture is like a smooth cream, then add the hazelnuts and run the machine for ½ minute more. Pour into a bowl, add the cheese, and mix. Beat the egg whites until very stiff. Gently fold the yolk mixture into the egg whites.

Butter the quiche pan, pour the batter into the pan, and bake in the 375° oven for 15 minutes. Then raise the oven heat to 425° and bake for another 15 minutes. Remove the cake from the oven and cool before unmolding. Refrigerate until ready to serve.

Serve with a fresh fruit salad.

Yield: 6 servings
Total calories: 1,475

Watermelon "Jello" with Blackberries

This is a refreshing summer dessert. What you need is ½ a watermelon, blackberries to simulate the watermelon seeds, and, if you can find them, some red currants to counter the sweetness of the watermelon. When I made this dessert, there was a lot of discussion around the table. Did it work? Was it tasty? Some said yes, others no, but they gobbled it down and asked for more. Try it and watch what happens.

½ watermelon
1 tablespoon lime juice
3 envelopes unflavored gelatin
3 tablespoons cold water
5 fresh mint leaves + extra for garnish
2 pints blackberries
1 pint red currants
2 tablespoons sugar

2-quart mold

Cut the melon into slices 4 inches thick, then each slice into quarters. With a fork remove all the seeds and scoop the red flesh out of the rind. Put the watermelon pieces in a food processor and run the machine until all the melon is puréed. (You should have about 4 cups.) Pour the purée into a large saucepan, add the lime juice, and heat gently. Meanwhile, soak the gelatin in a bowl with 3 tablespoons of cold water. Add the gelatin to the watermelon purée and stir until it is completely dissolved.

Arrange the 5 mint leaves in a flower pattern at the bottom of the mold, add 1 cup of the watermelon mixture, and refrigerate until it is set. Then add the blackberries to the remaining watermelon mixture and pour into the mold. Refrigerate for at least 2 hours. Carefully remove the red currants from their stems, rinse, and drain. Put the currants in a bowl with the sugar, toss, and refrigerate.

When ready to serve, plunge the bottom of the mold into hot water for a second, then unmold onto a round platter. Garnish with the currants and more fresh mint leaves.

Yield: 8 servings
Total calories: 1,585

Blueberry Cheese Cake

This cheese cake is very light for it is made with low-fat ricotta cheese and buttermilk. The topping could be a thin layer of raspberry purée or, as in this recipe, whole fresh blueberries.

4 cups low-fat ricotta cheese
4 eggs
1 cup buttermilk
½ cup honey
1 teaspoon salt
juice of 1 lemon + grated rind
2 teaspoons vanilla extract
1 teaspoon butter for the pan
1 pint blueberries
½ cup yogurt
1 tablespoon sugar

9½-inch springform pan, 2½ inches deep

Preheat the oven to 375°.

In a food processor place the cheese, eggs, buttermilk, honey, salt, lemon juice, lemon rind, and vanilla. Run the machine until all the ingredients are puréed and the mixture is smooth.

Butter the ring of the springform pan and pour the batter into the pan. Bake in a *bain-marie* (a pan of hot water) in the 375° oven for 45 minutes. Remove and cool at room temperature before refrigerating. Wash and drain the blueberries.

Just before serving, remove the ring of the springform pan. Beat together the yogurt and the sugar and spread in a thin coat over the top of the cake. Cover the cake with the blueberries.

Yield: 8 servings
Total calories: 2,620

Cake with Sliced Peaches

1 pound large ripe peaches
2 tablespoons brandy
1 lemon
6 tablespoons sugar
1 egg
⅔ cup flour
1 teaspoon baking soda
1½ teaspoons baking powder
½ cup yogurt
½ tablespoon butter for the pan
fresh mint leaves for garnish

9-inch pie pan

Peel, pit, and slice the peaches, put them in a bowl, add the brandy, and marinate for 1 hour.

Preheat the oven to 375°.

Grate the lemon zest and squeeze the lemon. In a food processor place the sugar and the egg, run the machine until the mixture is pale yellow, then add the flour, baking soda, and baking powder. Run the machine for ½ minute, then add the lemon zest, lemon juice, and yogurt. Run the machine until the batter is like a thick smooth cream.

Butter the pie pan, pour the batter into it, and bake in the 375° oven for 30 minutes or until the cake is golden brown. Unmold onto a plate and cool.

Garnish the top of the cake with the sliced peaches and arrange any leftover slices around the cake. Decorate with mint leaves.

Yield: 6 servings
Total calories: 1,120

Carrot-Orange Cake

1½ cups shredded carrots (about 4 carrots)
1 orange
1½ cups flour
2 teaspoons baking powder
½ teaspoon baking soda
1½ teaspoons cinnamon
½ teaspoon salt
¾ cup sugar
4 tablespoons melted butter
2 eggs
1½ teaspoons vanilla extract
juice of ½ lime
½ tablespoon butter for the pan

1-quart loaf pan

Preheat the oven to 350°.

Grate the orange rind and then squeeze the orange. Soak the grated carrots in the orange juice.

In a bowl mix together the flour, baking powder, baking soda, cinnamon, and salt. In another bowl mix together the sugar, melted butter, eggs, vanilla, and the orange rind. Add the egg mixture to the dry ingredients. Mix well, then add the lime juice.

Then add the carrots with the orange juice and mix well. Butter the loaf pan and pour in the cake batter. Bake in the 350° oven for 45 minutes or until a needle inserted in the center comes out clean. Cool before unmolding. Serve at room temperature.

Total calories: 2,000

Pumpkin Roll

3 eggs
1 cup sugar
⅔ cup canned pumpkin purée (about 8 ounces)
1 teaspoon lemon juice

2 teaspoons cinnamon
1 teaspoon grated fresh ginger
½ teaspoon nutmeg
½ teaspoon salt
1 tablespoon flour
1 teaspoon baking powder
¼ teaspoon butter for the pan
½ cup chopped walnuts

14-by-17-inch jelly-roll pan

Preheat the oven to 375°.

In a food processor place the eggs and sugar and run the machine until the eggs turn pale yellow. Add the pumpkin purée, lemon juice, spices, salt, flour, and baking powder. Run the machine until the ingredients are well mixed.

Butter the jelly-roll pan, cover it with wax paper, and spread the pumpkin batter on it. Bake in the 375° oven for 25 minutes or until a needle inserted comes out clean. Remove the cake from the oven and let cool. Starting at one short end, gently roll the cake away from the wax paper, like a jelly-roll. Sprinkle with the walnuts and press down on them gently. Serve at room temperature, with a fresh fruit salad.

Yield: 6 servings
Total calories: 1,590

Galette des Rois with Apricots

In France for Epiphany, we always serve a flat flaky pie, golden in color, which has a bean hidden inside. Whoever gets the bean is declared king or queen and has to choose his or her mate. This recipe is an adaptation because instead of hiding a bean in it I filled the *galette* with apricots.

½ pound dried apricots
3¼ cups flour
2 tablespoons sugar
¼ pound (1 stick) butter

pinch of salt
grated zest of 1 lemon
2 eggs + 1 yolk
½ tablespoon butter for the pan
2 tablespoons water

9-inch quiche pan

Preheat the oven to 425°.

Soak the apricots overnight in water. Drain them and purée in a food processor. Set aside in a bowl.

In the processor place the flour, sugar, the butter cut in small pieces, salt, lemon zest, and the 2 eggs. Run the machine until the dough forms a ball. Cut the ball of dough in two. On a floured board roll out ½ the dough about ⅛ inch thick.

Butter the quiche pan and line with the dough. Spread the apricot purée on top. Roll out the other half of the dough and place on top of the apricot filling. Roll the edges tightly.

Brush the top of the *galette* with the egg yolk first lightly beaten with 2 tablespoons water. Cook in the 425° oven until golden brown. Serve at room temperature, cut in wedges, with fresh fruit.

Yield: 8 servings
Total calories: 3,020

Gâteaux aux Biscuits

This recipe does have almost ¼ pound of butter in it. But if you have a simple dinner, you could indulge and have this cake. It can be frozen and served sliced as ice cream.

1 cup diced fresh fruit (peaches, melon, plums)
2 tablespoons rum
4 ounces ladyfingers + 3 for garnish
2 cups milk
6 egg yolks
3 tablespoons sugar
6 tablespoons butter + ½ tablespoon for the mold

1½-quart mold

Cut the fruit in ½-inch dice before measuring and place in a bowl with the rum. In another bowl crush the ladyfingers into large crumbs. Set aside.

In a saucepan heat the milk, but do not boil. In a food processor place the egg yolks and sugar. Run the machine until the eggs are pale yellow and then slowly add the hot milk. Pour the mixture back into the saucepan and cook over low heat, stirring all the time, until it is thick and smooth. Pour this custard into the bowl with the ladyfingers. Add the fruits and the 6 tablespoons butter, cut in small pieces. Mix well until all the butter is well incorporated into the mixture.

Butter the mold. Pour the mixture into the mold and refrigerate overnight. Unmold the *gâteau* onto a platter, crumble the remaining ladyfingers, and sprinkle them on top. Use a large spoon to serve the cake.

Yield: 6 servings
Total calories: 2,140

Prune Flan

In my family all the women love prunes, all the men hate them. But when I made this dessert, which had been taught to me by one of my great-aunts in Cairo, everyone agreed that prunes after all were sometimes quite good. The secret is the ¼ cup of armagnac in which the prunes have soaked overnight.

20 large prunes, pitted
¼ cup Armagnac
Pâte Brisée *(page 233)*
½ tablespoon butter for the pan
3 tablespoons flour
1 tablespoon salt
⅜ cup sugar
¼ cup milk
6 eggs

9-inch quiche pan

Soak the prunes overnight in the Armagnac.

Preheat the oven to 450°.

Roll out the pastry dough on a floured board. Line the buttered quiche pan with the dough.

In a food processor place the flour, salt, the sugar minus 1 tablespoon, and milk. Run the machine until the ingredients are well mixed, then add the eggs and whatever liquid is left from the soaked prunes. Run the machine again until all the ingredients are well mixed.

Arrange the prunes on the pastry dough and add the egg mixture. Lower the oven heat to 425° and bake the flan for 35 minutes or until a needle inserted in the center comes out clean. Remove from the oven, sprinkle with the remaining tablespoon of sugar, and serve immediately.

Yield: 6 servings
Total calories: 2,860

Mango Flan with Strawberries

2 mangoes
4 eggs
½ cup milk
4 fresh mint leaves
2 pints strawberries

4 individual soufflé dishes, 6-ounce capacity

Preheat the oven to 475°.

Peel the mangoes and cut the flesh away from the large center seed. In a food processor place the mangoes, eggs, and milk. Run the machine until all the ingredients are puréed. Pour the mixture into the soufflé dishes. Place a mint leaf on top of each, cover with foil, and bake in the 475° oven in a *bain-marie* (a pan of hot water) for 20 minutes or until a needle inserted in the center comes out clean. Cool, then refrigerate.

Meanwhile, hull the strawberries. Wash and drain. Purée half the berries in a food processor. Remove to a bowl. Garnish the flans with the remaining berries and serve the strawberry purée alongside.

Yield: 4 servings
Total calories: 955

Mango Mousse

Mangoes are one of my favorite fruits. When I was born, my father planted a mango tree under my bedroom window. By the time I was thirteen, it had reached the window and I knew everything there is to know about mangoes. In the mango season, my father used to take me to the market in Cairo; he taught me about the different types of mangoes (in Cairo there were at least five kinds), and all about chutney and mango juices. Here is one of the recipes that I liked the best.

2 large ripe mangoes
¾ cup yogurt
2 tablespoons orange liqueur
2 egg whites
½ lime for garnish

Peel the mangoes and cut the flesh away from the large center seed. In a food processor place the mangoes, yogurt, and orange liqueur and run the machine until the mangoes are puréed. Beat the egg whites until stiff, then gently fold in the mango purée. Pour the mixture into wineglasses and place in the freezer for ½ hour. Garnish each glass with ½ a lime slice.

Yield: 6 servings
Total calories: 535

Kiwi Custard

2 cups milk
6 eggs
1 cup sugar
¼ cup brandy
8 kiwis, peeled and sliced
1 pint raspberries or 1 package frozen raspberries

1½-quart mold

Preheat the oven to 375°.

In a saucepan heat the milk but do not let it boil. In a food processor place the eggs, sugar, brandy, and 2 of the sliced kiwis. Run the machine until the kiwis are puréed. With the machine still running, slowly add the hot milk.

Rinse the mold with cold water. Line the bottom and sides of the mold with the remaining slices of kiwi. Pour in the egg mixture. Bake the custard in a *bain-marie* (a pan of hot water) in the 375° oven for 25 to 30 minutes, or until it is set. Remove from the oven, let cool, then refrigerate for 3 to 4 hours.

Purée the raspberries. Unmold the custard onto a round platter and serve with the raspberry purée on the side.

Yield: 6 servings
Total calories: 2,345

Index